Barbados

by Lee Karen Stow

Award-winning travel journalist and photographer Lee Karen Stow travels widely and regularly for a number of national newspapers, magazines and adventure travel books. Lee lives in East Yorkshire, England.

Above: *Palm-fringed coral beaches on the sun-drenched west coast*

AA Publishing

A stilt walker on parade at a local carnival

Written by Lee Karen Stow

First published 2001
Reprinted May 2002
Reprinted March 2003
Reprinted 2004. Information updated and verified.
Reprinted May 2004, Aug 2004
Reprinted 2006. Information updated and verified.

Published by AA Publishing, a trading name of Automobile Association Developments Limited, whose registered office is Fanum House, Basing View, Basingstoke, Hampshire RG21 4EA. Registered number 1878835.

A02352
Atlas section and cover maps
© MAIRDUMONT/ Falk Verlag 2005

Colour separation: Keenes, Andover
Printed and bound in Italy by Printer Trento S.r.l.

Find out more about AA Publishing and the wide range of travel publicatons and services the AA provides by visiting our website at www.theAA.com/bookshop

Contents

About this Book

KEY TO SYMBOLS

✚ map reference to the maps found in the What to See section

✉ address or location

☎ telephone number

◷ opening times

🍴 restaurant or café on premises or nearby

🚌 nearest bus/tram route

⛴ ferry crossings and boat excursions

✈ travel by air

ℹ tourist information

♿ facilities for visitors with disabilities

✋ admission charge

↔ other places of interest nearby

❓ other practical information

▶ indicates the page where you will find a fuller description

This book is divided into five sections to cover the most important aspects of your visit to Barbados.

Viewing Barbados pages 5–10
An introduction to Barbados by the author.
    The 10 Essentials
    The Shaping of Barbados
    Peace and Quiet
    Barbados's Famous

Top Ten pages 11–22
The author's choice of the Top Ten places to see in Barbados, each with practical information.

What to See pages 23–72
The main areas of Barbados, each with its own brief introduction and an alphabetical listing of the main attractions.
    Practical information
    Snippets of "Did you know…"information
    3 suggested walks
    5 suggested drives
    5 special features

Where To… pages 73–86
Detailed listings of the best places to eat, stay, shop, take the kids and be entertained.

Practical Matters pages 87–93
A highly visual section containing essential travel information.

Maps
All map references are to the individual maps found in the What to See section of this guide.
For example, Oistins has the reference ✚ 24B1—indicating the page on which the map is located and the grid square in which the village is to be found. A list of the maps that have been used in this travel guide can be found in the index.

Prices
Where appropriate, an indication of the cost of an establishment is given by **$** signs:
$$$** denotes higher prices, **$$** denotes average prices, while **$ denotes lower charges.

Star Ratings
Most of the places described in this book have been given a separate rating:
✪✪✪   Do not miss
✪✪   Highly recommended
✪   Worth seeing

Viewing
Barbados

Above: *Bajans love life and are very laid back*
Right: *A Rastafarian sets up his easel on a west coast beach*

Lee Karen Stow's Barbados

A Coral Island

Barbados lies about 99 miles (160km) east of the Windward Islands. It grew out of the sea and is capped mostly by coral limestone, rising to a high point, Mount Hillaby, at 1,115ft (340m) above sea level. A mixed population of some 278,000 citizens is primarily of West African descent, followed by descendants of settlers from Great Britain. English is the official language.

Barbados enjoys a high repeat visitor factor, but it's not just sun, sea and sand that attracts holidaymakers. Barbadians are known to be among the friendliest people in the Caribbean and visitors who have found the soul of Barbados and forged friendships are those that have been coming back to the island for 20 years or more.

Barbados has gained a reputation as a celebrity hotspot. British Prime Minister Tony Blair heads an all-star cast of movie stars, supermodels and musicians who holiday in private villas and exclusive resorts along the West Coast.

Meanwhile, Barbados and its population of 278,000 carries on as it has done since tourism succeeded the sugarcane industry, drawing people to its good mix of attractions, natural formations of limestone caves and hidden guillies, and beautiful beaches lapped softly by ripples from the Caribbean Sea or swept by the crashing surf of the Atlantic. And to its glittering crop of restaurants and food shacks serving Bajan food and locally-produced rum and beer.

Despite nearly 40 years of independence from Great Britain, a quaint Englishness still exists with cricket on the green, horse-racing and afternoon tea. Enriching these traditions are African arts, crafts and songs—the roots unearthed by Bajans whose ancestors were brought here centuries ago, as slaves to work the sugar plantations.

In 2007 the Cricket World Cup comes to the island and the excitement is gathering pace. In the capital, Bridgetown, the Kensington Oval is being completely renovated into a state-of-the-art modern stadium. If you like all of the above, and cricket, you'll love Barbados.

Relaxing in a hammock on Almond Beach

THE **10** ESSENTIALS

If you only have a short time to visit Barbados, or would like to get a really complete picture of the country, here are the essentials:

• **Spend a day in Bridgetown** (➤ 26–33) shopping for tax-free jewelry, clothes and handicrafts, then stroll along the riverside boardwalk.

• **Snorkel with the turtles** on the west coast, or go diving to see them glide through the water (➤ 59).

• **Ride on an electric tram** through the limestone formations of Harrison's Cave (➤ 20), Barbados's most famous attraction.

• **Listen to gospel singing** and enjoy brunch at the Crane Beach Hotel (➤ 43), overlooking the dramatic Atlantic coast.

• **Eat fried flying fish and macaroni cheese pie** or rice at Oistins Fish Fry (➤ 51) on Friday and Saturday nights.

• **Take a picnic to Bathsheba** (➤ 15) on the east coast and watch the thunderous waves crash onto the cliffs.

• **Take a sunset cruise** and view Barbados from the water, or forget your cares on the lively Jolly Roger party cruise (➤ 83).

• **Visit a rum factory to learn how the national tipple is made**, then sample it and purchase a bottle to take home (➤ 49).

• **Dive to a depth of 147ft (45m) on the Atlantis Submarine** (➤ 57) to see a shipwreck, stingrays, turtles and shoals of colorful tropical fish—without getting wet.

• **Stroll through the terraces of plants** at the Andromeda Botanic Gardens (➤ 12–13), the extraordinary legacy of one woman.

Above: *Snorkelling with the inquisitive hawksbill turtles off the west coast*
Below: *Colorful printed beachwear for sale at Mullins Bay*

The Shaping of Barbados

c400 BC
Arawak Indians arrive by canoe from the coast of South America.

cAD 1200
The Caribs drive out the Arawaks.

1536
A Portuguese explorer lands and names the island Isla de los Barbados because of the bearded fig trees, or perhaps because the natives wore beards.

1625
English Captain John Powell arrives to find the island occupied by wild pigs. He claims it in the name of the English Crown. Two years later British settlers arrive. It is not known fully what happened to the Caribs.

1639
Barbados receives its first Parliament from the British Crown. British rule remains uninterrupted for the next 312 years.

1640–1807
Some 400,000 Africans are abducted from their homeland and forced to work as slaves in the Caribbean.

1807
Britain abolishes the slave trade but Barbados is slow to react.

Above: *slaves celebrate their freedom*
Right: *Owen Arthur*

1834
Abolition of slavery on Barbados is enacted, but not fully recognized until 1838.

1966
On November 30 full independence is granted. Barbados becomes an independent country within the British Commonwealth.

1975
Bajan cricket hero, Garfield Sobers is knighted.

1998
Prime Minister Owen Arthur declares National

Heroes Day on April 28.

2000
Barbados wins its first individual Olympic medal as Obadele Thompson captures bronze in the 100 metres final in Sydney, Australia.

2007
Barbados to host the Cricket World Cup.

Peace & Quiet

Escape to the isolated north and east coasts or to the nature parks and forests of the interior. A celebrated picnic spot at 898ft (274m), Farley Hill National Park (▶ 37) has views stretching across the Scotland District that tumbles to the Atlantic Ocean. Idle round the ruins of the old plantation house and weave through the Norfolk Island pines that flourish here.

Wildlife

Green monkeys thrive at the Barbados Wildlife Reserve (▶ 14), along with an imported python, iguanas and flamingos. The Graeme Hall Bird Sanctuary, a National Heritage Site, is the last of the island's mangrove swamps, now a nature reserve with a bird interpretation center, guided trails and walk-in aviaries with birds of the Lesser Antilles. Around 150 species of migratory bird, from North and South America, stop by on their way south, and it is hoped some species will stay. You can sit by one of four lakes and watch white cattle egrets jostle for branch space with little egrets.

Walking

Barbados's first fully-interactive guided trail, Arbib Nature and Heritage Trail (▶ 40) from Speightstown is split into two. The shorter walk is 3 miles (5.5km) whilst the longer, more arduous one is 5 miles (7.5km). Guides will distinguish flamboyant trees from cannonball trees for you and describe the medicinal uses of the island's plants. Every Sunday, the Barbados National Trust and Future Centre Trust run free hikes off the beaten track, ☎ 426 2421.

Keep an eye on the treetops for the Barbados green monkey

> ### DID YOU KNOW?
>
> Barbados was once smothered by forest, but the first colonizers managed to deforest the island in just 40 years. From the plane all you see is a flat, cultivated expanse, but the north has hills and small valleys, which you can reach by car or organized tour.

Barbados's Famous

Cricket

Cricketer Sir Garfield Sobers (1936–), known as the world's greatest all-rounder, is a legend on Barbados. He was knighted by Queen Elizabeth II in 1975, after scoring 8,032 runs and taking 235 wickets. The game itself, introduced by the British military and first played by whites in the 19th century, is now a national sport. Pakistan, Australia, England and other visiting teams descend upon the Kensington Oval in Fontabelle Road, Bridgetown—currently being updated to host the 2007 Cricket World Cup. The regional season runs from January to March. The international season takes place in June. Most days cricket is practised inside the Garrison Savannah racecourse—site of the earliest recorded matches.

Above: Home-grown cricket legend Sir Garfield Sobers

Rum

Barbados claims to be the home of rum and Mount Gay, owned by the Rèmy-Cointreau group, is the oldest brand in the world. Rum shops disguised as wooden shacks or colorful pubs are plentiful (around 1,000) and bottles to take home are cheap. Dark rum is aged in oak barrels, while white rum matures in modern vessels. The longer a rum has to age the better the taste. Visit the Heritage Park and Foursquare Rum Distillery (▶ 49) or Mount Gay Rum Distillery (▶ 50) and see how the liquor begins as juice extracted from molasses, a by-product of sugarcane. Tastings are often combined with a Bajan buffet.

Right: Mount Gay rum, said to be the oldest rum in the world

George Washington

In 1751, George Washington, America's first president, visited Barbados during the only trip he made outside the United States mainland. Aged 19, Washington traveled as a companion to his consumptive brother Lawrence, yet fell ill himself with smallpox. He stayed at Bush Hill House, in the Garrison Historic Area (▶ 19), scheduled to be restored by the Barbados National Trust.

Top Ten

Above: *Orchids at Orchid World*
Right: *Statue of Lord Nelson in National Heroes Square*

NELSON

11

1
Andromeda
Botanic Gardens

✚ 25C3

✉ Bathsheba, St. Joseph

☎ 433 9261 or 433 9384

🕐 Daily 9–5 (except public holidays)

🍴 Light meals, snacks and afternoon tea served at the Hibiscus Café ($$). The cook will also prepare a picnic lunch for you to eat in the gardens

🚌 From Bridgetown, Speightstown

♿ Good

✋ Moderate, children half price

↔ Bathsheba (► 15), Chalky Mount Village (► 17), Flower Forest and Orchid World (► 18)

❓ Further information from the Barbados National Trust, ☎ 426 2421

A profusion of both indigenous and tropical plants and flowers pays tribute to the mythical Greek goddess Andromeda in this garden by the ocean.

Bathsheba (► 15), on the rugged eastern coastline, makes a dramatic setting for this garden of color established in 1954 by the late amateur horticulturist Mrs Iris Bannochie. Iris devoted herself to the garden, creating

Tropical palms and plants flourish at Andromeda Botanic Gardens

trails of blossoms and tropical foliage on the cliffs above the Atlantic, and collected many rare species of plant on her trips around the world. She named her creation after the Greek maiden Andromeda (daughter of King Cepheus of Ethiopia) who, according to legend, was chained at the water's edge as a sacrifice to the sea monster before being rescued by Perseus.

Cascading streams and waterfalls have been added, and the gardens are building up a collection of medicinal plants with information on their traditional uses. Andromeda is astonishingly beautiful, awash with frangipani (*Plumeria rubra*), bougainvillaea (*Bougainvillea spectabilis*), traveler's trees (*Ravenala madagascariensis*) and orchids (*Orchidaceae*). Through strategically scattered palms you glimpse the azure blue of the ocean from viewpoints on the pathways. The fishing village in the distance is Tent Bay. As you admire Andromeda, Barbados monkeys swing in the trees above, and there are mongooses and lizards.

Quiet seclusion can be found at this garden by the ocean

In 1988, before her death, Iris donated her gardens to the Barbados National Trust. The Trust now offers guided tours led by knowledgeable volunteer horticulturists on Wednesdays at 10.30am. If you prefer to go it alone, there's a choice of two self-guided trails, one covering hilly areas and taking up to an hour, and the other a half-hour, easier stroll.

2
Barbados Wildlife Reserve

24B4

Farley Hill, St. Peter

422 8826

Daily 10–3.45

Café ($) serving snacks

Continuous bus service from Bridgetown, Holetown, Speightstown, Bathsheba

Good

Moderate, children half price. Includes admission to Grenade Hall Forest and Signal Station

Farley Hill National Park (➤ 37), Grenade Hall Forest and Signal Station (➤ 38), Morgan Lewis Sugar Mill (➤ 41)

Several sightseeing operators visit the reserve

DID YOU KNOW?

Some Barbadians consider the meat of the green monkey to be a delicacy.

This natural mahogany forest, home to exotic animals, birds and reptiles, also features buildings made of coral stone and relics of the sugar industry.

While sipping a cold drink at the mahogany bar within the reserve, don't be surprised to see a red-footed Barbados tortoise stroll by. Except for caged parrots and a python from the UK, the animals here generally roam freely over the 4 acres (1.5ha) of forest. The reserve is built from coral stone gathered from surrounding canefields and its paths are fashioned from bricks (that still carry the manufacturer's stamp) from 17th- and 18th-century sugar factories.

Children love it here, but they must be supervised as some of the animals, including the monkeys, can bite. Among the mix are cattle egrets, spectacled caimans, guinea fowl, deer, pelicans, congas, flamingos, cockatoos, toucans and peacocks. In a straw-carpeted pen, iguanas of the West Indies, the largest vertebrates native to the Caribbean islands, sprawl on logs. They bake in the sun, oblivious to the rabbits hopping around them and the juvenile tortoises crawling by. Many creatures arrived here as gifts to the reserve. The agoutis and the armadillos are from the forestry departments in St. Lucia and St. Vincent, while the pelicans hail from Florida.

To see the Barbados green (or vervet) monkeys, be here between 2 and 3pm, when the colony returns from the forests of nearby Grenade Hall. Originally introduced from West Africa, the monkey numbers around 5–7,000 on the island and just one animal can provide up to 2.5 million doses of polio vaccine. The reserve's Primate Research Centre, focusing on the use and conservation of the monkey, is responsible for up to 70 percent of the world's production of the vaccine.

A tortoise tucks into fruit at the Barbados Wildlife Reserve

3
Bathsheba

This tiny beauty spot on the east coast has a great appeal for those wanting to see the rugged, natural face of Barbados.

There are no luxury, fancy hotels at Bathsheba and you won't find anyone to park your car. Even in peak season, this fishing village is devoid of crowds. Its coves and bays are washed by excellent surf and surfing champions ride the waves from September to December at the frothy Soup Bowl at the center of the beach. Two rows of giant, grass-covered boulders seem to guard the bay from the threat of the approaching tide. In fact, apart from the bathing pools that fill up and can be enjoyed at low tide, it's far too dangerous to swim here.

✚ 25C3

🚌 Continuous bus service from Bridgetown, Holetown, Speightstown

🍴 Edgewater Inn (for Bajan buffet) ($)
✉ 433 9900

♿ None

↔ Andromeda Botanic Gardens (▶ 12–13), Chalky Mount Village (▶ 17)

What you can do, though, is stroll by the church and the pastel-painted houses or wander along the deserted beaches backed by chalky cliffs and wild hills. There are no formal attractions as such here, just the peace and scenery. Nearby are the green hills of Cattlewash, so-called because the cattle wander down to the sea to take a bath.

In Victorian times, Bathsheba was a magnet for holidaying Barbadians who would travel by train to take the air. A railroad ran from Bridgetown to Bathsheba from 1883 until it closed in 1937. Its life was precarious, suffering from landslides, underfunding and mismanagement. Coastal erosion was so bad the crew often had to alight to repair the track as they went.

Wild and natural, Bathsheba is renowned for its breathtaking beauty

4
Bridgetown, National Heroes Square

28B2

Junction of Broad Street and St. Michael's Row, Bridgetown, St. Michael

Numerous cafés and restaurants ($–$$) in Broad Street

All buses run to Bridgetown

None

Free

Parliament Buildings (➤ 30), Queen's Park (➤ 32), St. Michael's Cathedral (➤ 32)

Originally planned to represent London's Trafalgar Square in miniature, the capital's focal point is becoming increasingly Barbadian.

Before April 28, 1999, this main square was known as Trafalgar Square, a throwback to the days when Barbados was known as Little England. The square was renamed by the prime minister, Owen Arthur, in a ceremony that took place to mark the occasion of the second National Heroes Day. It is a holiday that remembers notable figures in the island's history.

During the ceremony, 10 people were honored, including Errol Walton Barrow, the first prime minister elected after independence in 1966; Bussa, the slave leader of the 1816 rebellion; cricket star Sir Garfield Sobers (➤ 10); and Samuel Jackman Prescod. Prescod, the son of a slave mother, rose in 1843 to become the country's first non-white member of Parliament in more than 200 years. He fought for the rights of all classes and colors.

A bronze statue of Lord Nelson was erected in the square in 1813. Nelson sailed to the island in 1805 with a large fleet, which included the *Victory*, months before he perished at the Battle of Trafalgar. For decades there's been talk of moving Nelson (he's considered as a defender of the slave trade) elsewhere and erecting a Barbadian figure, possibly that of Barrow, instead.

Opposite the admiral towers the obelisk honoring the Barbadians killed in World Wars I and II. In the center, the Dolphin Fountain commemorates the first running water piped to the town. Surrounding the square are the neo-Gothic buildings of the seat of Parliament, including Treasury and House of Assembly (➤ 30). This is an ideal starting point for your own walking tour of the capital.

The Dolphin Fountain in National Heroes Square, backed by the Parliament Buildings

5
Chalky Mount Village

You can watch pottery being made and fired traditionally and enjoy fabulous views of the Scotland District in the chalk hills of St. Andrew.

Winston Paul at the wheel of Highland Pottery at Chalky Mount Village

The skilled potter Winston Junior Paul and his wife, Prim, run Highland Pottery, a uniquely placed workshop high in Chalky Mount Village. It stands on a geological formation said to resemble a sleeping man with his hands folded over his stomach. Locals refer to it as "Napoleon." At one time over 20 pottery businesses thrived here, the studios and workshops humming in wood houses high on the hills. Today, only a couple struggle to make a living, battling against cheap imports. Beneath them is the brown-red clay dug to create the artists' pieces. Winston's workshop is like a tree-house, open on all sides to let in the refreshing breezes. It has a 360-degree view of the undulating eastern landscape, known as the Scotland District, that rambles down to the Atlantic.

Winston tells you how the clay is first mixed with water then sieved to take out the tree roots. The mixture is then laid out on drying trays in the sun for about three weeks until the water has evaporated. Next it is brought indoors where the rushing wind dries out the last of the water. He invites you to watch him knead the clay on the wedging table, squeezing out the bubbles before slapping it down on the potter's wheel. Before the advent of electricity, pots were thrown on a kick wheel, which is made of cement and shaped like a millstone. The wheel is kicked to rotate the clay and Winston is so skilled at it that he appears to be running while shaping a flower vase before your eyes. He then fires the pots in the kiln, after which they are painted and glazed and displayed on shelves.

✚ 24B3

✉ Chalky Mount Potteries, Chalky Mount, Scotland District

☎ Telephone to be installed, Winston can be reached on 422 9818

🕐 Daily 9–5

🍴 Restaurants/cafés ($–$$) at Bathsheba

🚌 From Bridgetown

♿ None

🎟 Free

↔ Andromeda Botanic Gardens (► 12–13), Bathsheba (► 15)

6
Flower Forest and Orchid World

This colorful duo, featuring tropical and native trees and spectacular orchids, lies on a popular scenic route in the parishes of St. Joseph and St. John.

Flower Forest

✚ 24B3

✉ Richmond, St. Joseph

☎ 433 8152

🕐 Daily 9–5 (last tour 4pm)

🍴 On site café ($)

🚌 From Bridgetown take the Chalky Mount or Sugar Hill bus and ask the driver to drop you off near the forest

♿ Good

✋ Moderate

↔ Harrison's Cave (► 20), Welchman Hall Gully (► 72)

Orchid World

✚ 24C2

✉ Between Gun Hill and St. John's Church, Highway 3b

☎ 433 0306

🕐 Daily 9–5 (last admission 4.30)

🍴 Café ($)

🚌 From Bridgetown take the Sargeant Street bus

♿ Good

✋ Moderate

↔ Gun Hill Signal Station (► 71)

Flower Forest
Set 846ft (258m) above sea level on a former sugar plantation, the forest has a visitor center furnished with old copper sugar-boiling vats and decorated with a mural depicting the plantation's history. From here a self-guided nature trail leads through a tropical corridor of neatly labeled plants and trees. Look out for the native bearded fig tree (*Ficus citrifolia*), bamboos and breadfruit (*Artocarpus altilis*), plus the Queen of Flowers tree, which was planted by Princess Alexandra in 1992. Some rest spots overlook manicured lawns, the most splendid being Liv's Lookout, with views to the rugged Scotland District and the island's highest point, Mount Hillaby, at 1,115ft (340m).

Orchid World
Opened by Prime Minister Owen Arthur in 1998, Orchid World lies in the high rainfall sector of the island, which averages 79in (203cm) annually. Rainwater is collected in a 29,920-gal (136,000-L) tank and, so far as is possible, recycled. This makes for a healthy environment for a plethora of orchid species that is continually being added to. Orchids spring up everywhere, and *vandas*, *schomburgkia* and *oncidium* grow by the paths. *Epiphytes*, or air plants, dangle from wire frames in the specially controlled environment of the orchid houses. Coral, limestone rockeries, caves and a babbling stream add to the tranquillity of the garden, which has a far-reaching view across the silvery sheen of the sugarcane fields.

Above: Many different species of orchid color the green tranquillity of Orchid World

7

Garrison Historic Area

Once the defence nucleus of Barbados, the Garrison comprises a circle of mid-17th century military buildings and an exceptional cannon collection.

When Oliver Cromwell took control of England after the Civil War of 1648, he set his sights on Barbados. But Lord Willoughby, the governor of Barbados, decided to strengthen the island's defence and provide the existing military with arms. Needham's Fort, later renamed Charles Fort, today stands as the oldest building, dating back to 1650. It was strengthened by the addition of another fort, St. Ann's, which is now the headquarters of the Barbados Defence Force.

When France declared war on Britain in 1778, an influx of British troops arrived at the Garrison. The bewildered Barbados government, who had trouble finding enough accommodations for them, were forced to build temporary barracks. The majority of troops left when the war ceased, but for those that stayed, and to dissuade future attacks on British islands in the Caribbean, a permanent Garrison building was constructed.

Over the years the Garrison has witnessed many alterations. The distinctive redbrick clocktower of the Main Guard has changed little. The 30 or so 17th- to 18th-century cannons, from reputedly the largest collection in the world, will soon be moved to St. Ann's Fort.

Since the withdrawal of the British troops from Barbados in 1905/6, some buildings have been refurbished. The latest to receive attention is Bush Hill House where the United States' first president, George Washington, stayed in 1751. St. Ann's Fort and the Main Guard are also being restored.

Horse-racing takes place on the Garrison Savannah, the former parade ground. By day cricket teams practise their batting and fielding, while locals jog around the track. It was here, on November 20, 1966, that the British Union Flag was lowered and Barbados's blue and gold flag—bearing a trident—raised to mark Independence Day.

✝ 24B1

✉ St. Michael

🍴 Brown Sugar ($$)

🚌 From Bridgetown and the south coast

♿ Few

✋ Free

↔ Bridgetown (➤ 26), Barbados Museum (➤ 34)

❓ 1½-hour tours around the Garrison area. Own transport needed. ☎ 427 1436

Part of the Garrison's cannon, soon to be moved to St. Ann's Fort

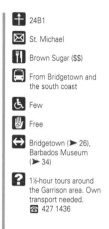

8
Harrison's Cave

✛ 24B3

✉ Welchman Hall, St. Thomas

☎ 438 6640

 Tours daily at half-hourly intervals. First tour 9.30, last tour 4

🍴 Snack bar ($–$$) on site

🚌 Bus from Bridgetown marked Shorey Village

♿ Few

✋ Moderate

 Welchman Hall Tropical Forest (► 72)

A ride on an electric tram takes you through the subterranean stream passages of a natural limestone wonder—the island's most famous site.

A labyrinth of creamy white stalagmites and stalactites dripping with rainwater, Harrison's Cave is a world away from the tropical jungle above it. Deep below the island's geographical center, you don a hard hat and hop aboard a trolley car for a 1-mile (1.5-km) long guided tour. Following a smooth underground passageway, you halt to photograph the "cathedral" chamber, a waterfall pouring into a 8-ft (2.5-m) deep pool. Nearby is a group of conical shapes known as "people's village." Alongside runs the original subterranean stream. Above hangs the 'chandelier,' continuously dripping with calcite-laden water. The stalactites and stalagmites have been growing over thousands of years and in some places have joined together to form pillars.

First discovered in 1796 by Dr George Pinckard, an

Stalactites meet stalagmites in the dramatic caverns of Harrison's Cave

English doctor who lived on the island, the cave was rediscovered in 1970 by a Danish speleologist and a Barbadian caver. It was brought to the attention of the government and work on creating an attraction began. Explorations and excavations followed and an underground stream was diverted. The first tourists arrived in 1981 and the cave has since welcomed Queen Elizabeth II and musicians Paul McCartney and Elton John. The full story of the caves and how they were discovered is via an audio visual show in a special theater, shown before the tour gets underway. The cave is one of the island's "must see" sights.

9
Speightstown

Brightly colored fishing boats, wooden houses and a quaint church make up this typical West Indian haunt, Barbados's second biggest town.

Speightstown (pronounced "Spitestown") might appear sleepy, but the calm is broken when the fishing boats come in and locals arrive to shop. It bears a history as a thriving port for sugar and the old commercial part with its surviving colonial architecture, notably the Georgian balconies, is gradually being restored by the Barbados National Trust.

The town offers modern shopping in the Mall, bakeries serving Bajan bread, and market stalls of fruit and vegetables. There's also the chance to while away the hours in a rum shop with the Bajans on a Saturday afternoon, listening to cricket on the local radio.

Founded by William Speight, Speightstown earned the name Little Bristol after Bristol in England, which was the principal export destination for the island's sugar. Because of Speightstown's importance, military forts were built around it for protection but today very little remains of this defensive ring.

St. Peter's Parish Church, one of the earliest churches on the island, originally dates from around 1630. Inside, the wooden gallery above was once occupied by the "poor whites," the name given to descendants of English, Irish and Scots who were imported as indentured labour to work on the sugarcane plantations.

A "Round de Town" stroll (► panel) and the award winning Arbib Nature and Heritage Trail (► 40), organized by the Barbados National Trust, begin by the painted blue benches at the harborside, just past the Fisherman's pub. If you're early enough, you will catch Bajans dozing on the benches and the cobbler setting out his tools for a day's shoe mending.

✚ 24A4

✉ Speightstown, St. Peter

🚌 Buses from all over the island

♿ Few

↔ West Coast (► 58)

❓ A 2-hour "Round de Town" stroll runs on Wed and Sat (or by alternative arrangement) from 9am or 2.30pm, depending on numbers, with the Barbados National Trust ☎ 234 9010 💲 Moderate, children half price

Fruit stalls line a side street in Speightstown

10
Sunbury Plantation House

Sunbury revels in the history of the sugarcane boom

Bordered by gardens, this 340-year-old plantation house is crammed to the ceiling with relics from the days of the great white sugar planters.

✚ 25C2

✉ St. Philip

☎ 423 6270

🕐 Daily 9.30–4.30

🍴 Courtyard restaurant and bar ($–$$)

🚌 From Oistins to College Savannah or Bayfield

♿ None

✋ Moderate

↔ Crane Beach Hotel (➤ 43), Sam Lord's Castle (➤ 44)

❓ A planter's candlelit dinner at Sunbury's 200-year-old mahogany table includes a five-course meal, cocktails, unlimited drinks and a tour of the house. Reservations required. Minimum number of 10.

For the best insight into how the wealthy white planters lorded it up while their slaves and laborers sweated with the sugarcane, step across the threshold of Sunbury Plantation House. You're immediately surrounded by trappings of the rich, an outstanding collection of Victorian and Edwardian pottery, silverware and china. Anywhere else such a trove would be roped off or protected behind glass show cabinets. At Sunbury, where all the rooms are accessible, you walk among the Barbados mahogany tables and antiques as though you're waiting for the owner to return from his harvest.

Originally thought to be called Chapmans after one of the first planter families, Sunbury is now owned by Mr and Mrs Keith Melville of Barbados. They opened the house to the public in 1983.

Highlights include the sunroom, furnished with a white rattan suite, where the ladies would mingle. Men conducted business in the office, the only room to contain the house's original oddments, including a 1905 calculator. Portraits of wealthy landowners hang alongside drawings of scenes from the West Indies during the days of slavery. Upstairs, the airy bedrooms are a treat. Check out the 1920s swimming costume, the marble hip bath and the lady's silver brush set on the dressing table. Down in the cellar you'll find a range of saddlery and domestic appliances, plus a collection of horse-drawn carriages.

What To See

PARISH OF St PHILIP

X MILES TO BRIDGE TOWN

G. FLETCHER LONDON

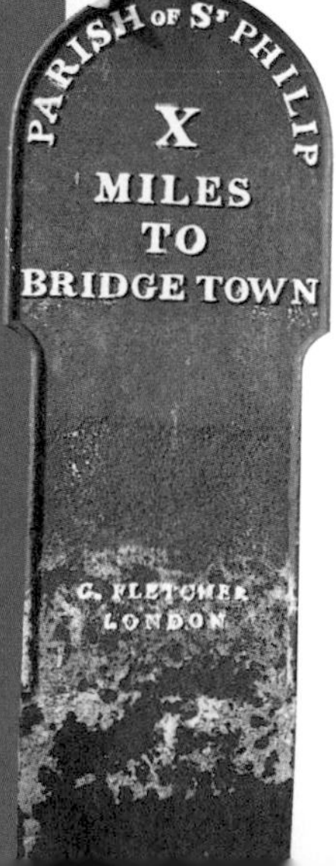

Above: *Take the helicopter for a bird's eye view of Barbados*
Right: *A road sign, a relic of colonial times, now at Sunbury Plantation House*

23

A salad bowl of produce for sale at a Bridgetown street stall

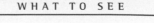

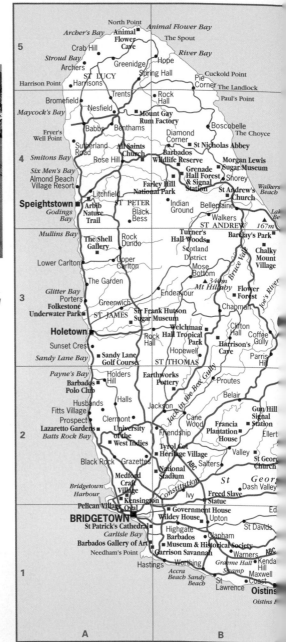

BARBADOS

0   2   4   6 km

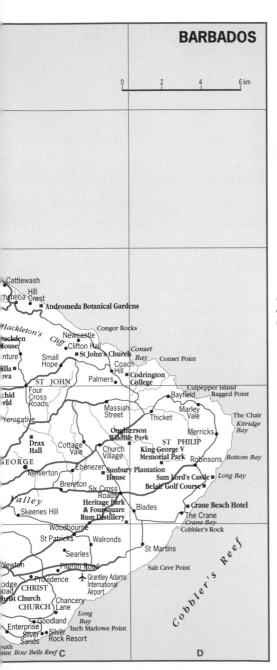

Cattlewash
Hill
chgheba Crest
■ **Andromeda Botanical Gardens**

Hackleton's Congor Rocks
uckden *Cliff* Newcastle
louse Clifton Hall
nture Small ■ **St John's Church** *Conset*
Hope Coach *Bay* Conset Point
illa ■ Hill ■ **Codrington**
va Palmers **College**
ST JOHN
chid Four Culpepper Island
rld Cross Bayfield Ragged Point
Roads
Massiah The Chair
rerogative Street Thicket Marley *Kitridge*
Vale *Bay*
Drax Oughterson Merricks
Hall Cottage **Wildlife Park**
EORGE Vale Church **ST PHILIP**
Melverton Village **King George V**
Ebenezer **Memorial Park** Robinsons *Bottom Bay*
Sunbury
Brereton **House** **Sam Lord's Castle** ■ *Long Bay*
Six Cross **Belair Golf Course** ■
Valley Roads
Skeenes Hill **Heritage Park** Blades ■ **Crane Beach Hotel**
& Foursquare The Crane
Woodbourne **Rum Distillery** *Crane Bay*
St Patricks Walronds Cobbler's Rock
lewton Searles St Martins
Pilgrim Road
odge ●Providence ✈ Grantley Adams Salt Cave Point
oad **CHRIST** International
hrist Church Chancery Airport
CHURCH Lane
Enterprise Goodland *Long*
Silver ● Silver *Bay*
Sands Rock Resort Inch Marlowe Point
outh
int *Bow Bells Reef* **C** **D**

*Bougainvillea grows in
abundance on the
island*

25

Bridgetown

When a cruise ship docks at Bridgetown's state-of-the-art cruise passenger terminal, the town is packed. This major duty free port in the Caribbean offers cut-price perfumes, tobacco and spirits, which prompts passengers to whizz round with credit cards and slip in a helicopter flight before jumping back on board to say they've done Barbados. Long after the cruise ships have pulled up anchor, though, you can people-watch in a café by the refurbished waterfront or haggle at the Rastafarian market. You can bet on the next horse-race, watch cricket on the green, or photograph the ramparts of a 17th-century fort. Bridgetown is the busiest place on Barbados, awash with tourists and locals, office workers with mobile phones, streetsellers and hooting cars. A day and a night are enough for a quick look and taste.

> *"(the men)... enlisted in the Barbados Volunteer Force were called into the barracks at the Garrison, to live and prepare themselves for the defence of the British Empire, and to eat bully-beef and biscuits. "*
>
> AUSTIN CLARKE
> *Growing Up Stupid Under the Union Jack*
> (1980)

Bridgetown

The town was originally known as Indian River Bridge, after the discovery of an Amerindian bridge that spanned the Constitution River here. Founded by British settlers in 1628, it grew up to become the island's administrative and commercial capital and principal port. Before independence in 1966 Bridgetown bowed under British sovereignty, which is why you'll detect traces of English character in its colonial architecture, notably the Parliament Buildings (➤ 30) in National Heroes Square (➤ 16), the Garrison's military forts (➤ 19), a statue of Lord Nelson and a splendid racecourse. Bridgetown, with the sumptuously furnished houses of the sugar planters and warehouses stocked with goods from around the globe, was compared to wealthy Port Royal in Jamaica before the latter was wiped out by an earthquake.

A hired Mini Moke negotiates the Bridgetown traffic

The bulk of Barbados's 278,000 population lives in and around the capital, with an estimated 100,000 actually within the city and suburbs. The capital is the seat of the Barbados government, with the British monarch holding executive powers and represented on the island by a governor general, who in turn advises the cabinet and appoints the prime minister. Next come 21 members of the Senate and a 28-member House of Assembly, residing in the Parliament Buildings.

Most of the attractions can be seen in half a day on a walking tour starting near National Heroes Square (➤ 31), with the rest of the day spent shopping and trying out the cafés and restaurants. Bridgetown is also a base for day cruises, yacht charters, a trip on the Atlantis Submarine (➤ 57) and scenic helicopter flights.

What to See in Bridgetown

THE CAREENAGE ○○

Alongside the Careenage—a narrow inner harbor at the mouth of the Constitution River—a wooden boardwalk dressed with ornate, green-painted street lamps takes you past dozens of charter yachts and ocean-going boats advertising tours and deep-sea fishing. On the other side of the harbor are the many restored and painted houses of The Wharf. Towards the town, the boardwalk leads back to the main square or across Chamberlain Bridge to Independence Arch. Built in 1987, this monument commemorates the 21st anniversary of the island's independence.

 28B2

☒ The Wharf, off National Heroes Square

🍴 Waterfront cafés ($–$$)

🚌 Fairchild Street, main bus terminal

♿ Few

🎫 Free

Perfect for strolling, the lamp-lit walkway along the Careenage in Bridgetown

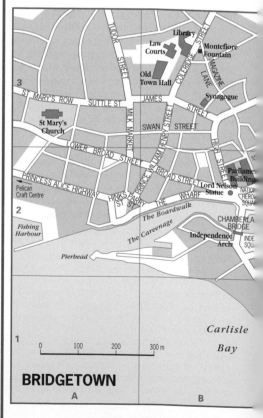

BRIDGETOWN

JEWISH SYNAGOGUE ✪✪

Tucked away off Magazine Lane and worth a visit is the Jewish Synagogue. Next door is a Jewish cemetery where weathered tombs contain the remains of Jews who arrived in Bridgetown in the 17th century and set up businesses in nearby Swan Street. The synagogue dates back to 1654, but was rebuilt in the 19th century following extensive hurricane damage. Remarkably well kept by the Barbados National Trust, it is likely to be one of the oldest synagogues in the western hemisphere. Inside, gorgeous wood paneling is brightened by the light from a quartet of brass chandeliers. Members of the island's present Jewish population still use the synagogue on a regular basis.

✚ 28B3
✉ Synagogue Lane, off Magazine Lane
☎ Barbados National Trust, 426 2421
🕐 Mon–Fri 9–12, 1–4
🚌 Fairchild Street
♿ Few
✋ Free, donations welcome

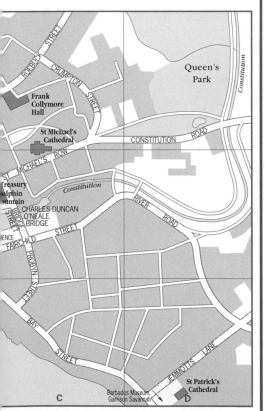

The chandelier and mahogany interior of the Jewish Synagogue in Bridgetown

28B3
Coleridge Street
Fairchild Street
None
Free

MONTEFIORE FOUNTAIN ✪

The Montefiore Fountain, built in memory of a Jewish businessman called John Montefiore, was originally installed in Beckwith Place. Its position today, on what looks like a traffic island in Coleridge Street, seems inappropriate for such a beauty. Look closely and you'll see the figures of Fortitude, Temperance, Patience and Justice portrayed. The accompanying inscription reads, "Look to the end; Be sober-minded; To bear is to conquer; Do wrong to no one."

NATIONAL HEROES SQUARE (➤ 16, TOP TEN)

28B2
Top of Broad Street
426 3717
Open by appointment
Fairchild Street
None
Moderate

Built in memory of a Jewish businessman, the Montefiore Fountain

PARLIAMENT BUILDINGS ✪✪

Though Barbados has the third oldest parliament in the Commonwealth, established in 1639 with an all-white House of Assembly, the Parliament Buildings to the north of National Heroes Square are younger. This is due to the number of fires that blighted the town, the most devastating occurring in 1766. Following the fire of 1860, the Parliament Buildings you see now were built in neo-Gothic style. This group includes the Senate and the House of Assembly, the latter fitted with stained-glass windows depicting British monarchs and Oliver Cromwell. The clock-tower is not the original; that was demolished in 1884 and a new one built two years later. Here sat the decision-makers, colonists of the 1700s busily reaping the rewards of sugarcane farming. You can imagine them fretting over whether the "mother country," England, would interfere with their right to self-government, or whether their slaves were plotting to rebel. Take an organized tour of the Open Gallery to see the stained-glass windows, a speaker's chair—a gift from the Indian government at independence—and a mace.

Around Bridgetown

Begin at National Heroes Square (▶ 16) and take the left arm along St. Michael's Row for a look in St. Michael's Cathedral (▶ 32).

Carry on up St. Michael's Row until you reach the gates of Queen's Park (▶ 32).

Stroll through the grounds, peer into the Georgian house, and find the African baobab tree.

Head back to National Heroes Square by the same route and turn right up Marthill Street. The road veers left and then right onto Magazine Lane.

You'll soon come to Synagogue Lane to the left, which leads to the Jewish Synagogue (▶ 29) and, behind a low wall to the right of the building, the Jewish cemetery.

Return to Magazine Lane, turning left towards the Montefiore Fountain (▶ 30).

Behind the fountain are the law courts, library and police station. Until they were closed in 1878, the law courts housed the Town Hall Gaol. Behind is Tudor Street, one of the oldest streets in the city.

Carry on southwestwards along Coleridge Street, turning right into Swan Street. At the junction with Milk Market turn left and continue until you reach the throng of Broad Street.

Once known as New England Street, Broad Street is Bridgetown's main thoroughfare, lined with stores selling duty-free jewelry, rums, perfumes, leather goods and other tourist goods. An eyecatcher is the sugary pink-and-white Victorian facade of Da Costa's Mall.

At this point you can either take a detour right and stroll along the boardwalk around The Careenage (▶ 28), or continue to the starting point of the walk near the Nelson statue.

Distance
Approx 1.25 miles (2km)

Time
3 hours or half a day with lunch, shopping and rest stops

Start/End Point
National Heroes Square
🔲 28B2
✉ Fairchild Street

Lunch
Bean-n-Bagel ($)
✉ The Wharf, Bridgetown
☎ 436 7778
🕐 Mon–Sat 7–4.30

Pretty pink Victorian facade of Da Costa's Mall in Broad Street

✚ 29D3
✉ End of St. Michael's Row
⊘ Daily
🚌 Fairchild Street
♿ None
🖐 Free

Above: *The tree-flanked entrance to St. Michael's Cathedral in Bridgetown*

✚ 29C3
✉ St. Michael's Row
☎ 427 0790
⊘ Daily 9–5
🚌 Fairchild Street
♿ Few
🖐 Free, donations welcome

Opposite: *Decorative stained-glass windows in St. Michael's Cathedral*

QUEEN'S PARK ★

One of the attractions in the park is the 89-ft (27-m) high baobab, estimated to be 1,000 years old and believed to have originated in Guinea, West Africa. Its circumference is 82ft (25m). In the pleasant park surrounding the baobab you'll see Barbadians in suits resting for lunch and children playing on the steps of the bandstand. The white Georgian building, Queen's Park House, was once the home of the commander of the British troops. It is now devoted to exhibitions of local arts and the theater.

ST. MICHAEL'S CATHEDRAL ★

The cathedral began as a small wooden church with enough seats for a 100-strong congregation. It was built between 1660 and 1665, but was destroyed by a hurricane in 1780 and had to be rebuilt from scratch. The new St. Michael's became a cathedral when William Hart Coleridge, the first bishop of the island, arrived on Barbados in 1825.

> ### DID YOU KNOW?
>
> Barbados has one of the highest literacy rates in the world, with 98 percent of the population able to read and write. All children attend school and are unmistakable in their smart uniforms.

LORD NOW LETTEST THOU THY
SERVANT DEPART IN PEACE

HE WAS RECEIVED UP INTO HEAVEN
AND SAT ON THE RIGHT HAND OF GOD

THIS IS MY BELOVED SON IN
WHOM I AM WELL PLEASED

TO THE GLORY OF GOD AND IN
DEC 24 1888 THIS WINDOW

MEMORY OF THE HON JAMES
IS ERECTED BY HIS SON

ALSOP LYNCH M.L.C WHO DIED
JAMES CHALLONER LYNCH

What to See Around Bridgetown

24B1

St. Ann's Garrison, St. Michael

427 0201

Mon–Sat 9–5 (except public hols), Sun 2–6

Many cafés nearby

Fairchild Street, or from the south alight at Garrison Savannah

Good

Inexpensive

Specially designed tours can be arranged. A Fine Craft Festival, featuring local art and craft, is held on the first Sat in Dec

Gateway to the island's history at the Barbados Museum

BARBADOS MUSEUM AND HISTORICAL SOCIETY ✪✪

A non-profit-making institution, the Barbados Museum and Historical Society provides a wonderfully old-fashioned introduction to Barbados. Around 250,000 objects, including West Indian fine and decorative arts, pre-Columbian archaeological pieces and African objects, are contained within its walls.

Displays begin with the evolution of the planet and a showcase of specimen coral, a major ecosystem of the island. Tools fashioned from coral by the Arawaks and Caribs are here, as are explanations of the tribes' religious beliefs. Fast-forward to the 1600s and you come to the arrival of the English colonists. From 1627 to 1640, until sugarcane florished, tobacco and cotton were the main crops. Planters relied heavily on African slaves to develop the sugar economy and it is estimated that around 400,000 slaves were imported to Barbados between 1627 and 1807. Their skin was stamped with the initials of their white owner, using an instrument similar to the museum's silver slave-brand dated *c*1800. The museum explains how, after emancipation, slaves tried to make the transition to independent peasantry through schooling, farming, entertainment and music.

Outside are examples of the island's architecture and a military gallery with the uniform of the Barbados yeoman guard. Prints showing the days of slavery, bequeathed to the museum by shipping magnate Sir Edward Cunard,

hang in a gallery also graced with shell displays. The African Gallery is now open and redesigned to link the Caribbean with its African ancestry. Of fascinating importance is a collection of rare West Indian books, plus early maps of Barbados including the earliest known map, dated 1657.

A curtain of home-made leather and coconut shell souvenirs

GARRISON HISTORIC AREA (▶ 19, TOP TEN)

PELICAN CRAFT CENTRE ✪
Sitting on land reclaimed from the sea, the center's pyramidal roofs shelter shops selling local arts and crafts. It also has workshops where you can watch some of Barbados's finest craftspeople at work. Metalwork, glassware, wooden crafts, pottery, paintings and batiks come with a reasonable price tag. You can also buy Royal Barbados Cigars made by the Caribbean Cigar Company. Sometimes a steel band is playing or a cultural dance is enacted. You can easily spend half a day here. There is a restaurant, and a café serves breakfast, lunch and afternoon drinks with a varied menu of pastries, fish, meat and poultry. Occasional shows are held during the year, especially around Christmas.

- 🪧 24A1
- ✉ Princess Alice Highway, Bridgetown
- ☎ 426 0765
- 🕐 Mon–Fri 10–5, Sat 9–2. Hours extend during peak holiday season
- 🍴 Cork and Bottle Café ($)
- ♿ Few
- 🎟 Free

ST. PATRICK'S CATHEDRAL ✪
The cornerstone of Roman Catholic St. Patrick's Cathedral was originally laid in 1840, but because of lack of funds and too few Catholics, it wasn't consecrated until decades later, in 1899. The interior is dressed with Scottish marble, Irish crests and flags. Nearby, overlooking the Esplanade and Carlisle Bay, is a statue of social reformer and former prime minister Sir Grantley Adams. He stands outside the present government's headquarters and offices of the prime minister.

- 🪧 29D1
- ✉ Highway 7, St. Michael
- 🕐 Daily
- 🍴 Many choices ($–$$) on the coastal road
- 🚌 Take buses to Bridgetown or the south coast
- ♿ Few
- 🎟 Free, donations welcome

Around the Island

Heavily settled by Arawak Indians, who harvested the rich fishing grounds, the north is the least developed part of the island today. Millions of blades of sugarcane, silvery in the sunlight, bend towards the white surf that crashes onto craggy North Point. Similarly unspoilt is the breathtaking east coast, with the hilly Scotland District plunging down to sand and palm beaches.

The south and west are the tourist hubs, each very different in character—and price. Rising up to the highlands in the center are patches of tropical forest above limestone caves.

It's possible to drive around the whole island in one day, but you'd be wiser exploring sections at a time and taking a long lunch, out of the midday heat. Alternatively, round up some friends and hire a cab, or book an organized tour. The beauty of Barbados is that wherever you are, a beach is never far away.

> *"In plenty and in time of need*
> *When this fair land was young*
> *Our brave forefathers sowed the seed*
> *From which our pride is sprung."*

IRVING BURGIE
Barbados National Anthem (1966)

●

What to See in the North

ANIMAL FLOWER CAVE ✪✪

The cave is at North Point, which is as far north as you can go on Barbados. Expect a breezy and exposed, yet fabulous, spot for photography. Steps lead down to a cavern carved out of the coral rock where there are scattered pools filled with sea anemones. Natural historian Griffith Hughes described them as animal flowers in 1750. Look behind you and the view of the ocean is amazing. Look down and you'll notice the pools are deep enough to swim in, but be careful of the slippery surface. The beauty of the cave prompted international singing star Billy Ocean to feature it in one of his pop music videos.

BARBADOS WILDLIFE RESERVE (➤ 14, TOP TEN)

FARLEY HILL NATIONAL PARK ✪

Once the most imposing mansion on Barbados, 19th-century Farley Hill at Farley Hill National Park was built to show off the accumulated wealth of the sugar planters. Originally known as Grenade Hall, it came into the hands of Sir Thomas Graham Briggs, who named it Farley Hill. Amid the fire-damaged ruins, overgrown with plants, you can imagine the sumptuous parties held here during the heyday of the sugar boom. Prince Alfred, the second son of Queen Victoria, and Prince George (later George V of England) arrived in carriages to take luncheon or dinner. Though you can't enter the roofless house for safety reasons, you can get a good look at the ruins through its windowless frames. The park trail leads to a picnic spot overlooking the Scotland District and Atlantic coastline where you might hear the rustle of green monkeys in the treetops above.

✚	24A5
✉	St. Lucy
☎	439 8797
🕐	Daily 9.30–5
🍴	Café ($) serving snacks
🚌	From Bridgetown take the Connell town bus
♿	Good 🖐 Inexpensive

Above: *The spectacular view from the anemone-scattered Flower Cave*
Below: *Roses spring up between the ruined walls of Farley Hill mansion*

✚	24B4
✉	St. Peter
☎	422 3555
🕐	Daily 8.30–5
🍴	Café ($) at Barbados Wildlife Reserve opposite
🚌	From Bridgetown, Speightstown, Bathsheba
♿	Good 🖐 Inexpensive

The restored 19th-century tower of the Grenade Hall Signal Station

✚ 24B4
✉ Farley Hill, St. Peter
☎ 422 8826
🕐 Daily 10–5, last entry 3.30–3.45 (arrive before 3 to see the monkeys)
🚌 From Speightstown
♿ Good
🖐 Moderate; includes Forest and Signal Station

GRENADE HALL FOREST AND SIGNAL STATION ★★

This is a good place to escape the relentless Caribbean sun. A trail descends through a web of vines and winds on for nearly a mile on paved paths smothered in moss. It's slippery, so wear strong soles with treads. At intervals you'll see questions (forming part of a quiz), plus quotes and anecdotes from the likes of Charles Darwin and an Amerindian chief. These remind us that man continues to rape the rainforests of the world for timber. There is a cave that sheltered Arawak Indians and, later, Rastafarians and escaped convicts. Shell tools found here are on display at the Barbados Wildlife Reserve (➤ 14).

Next door to the forest is the restored, whitewashed tower of the Grenade Hall Signal Station, built in 1819. Barbados had a string of such stations, established following the slave rebellion of 1816. During the uprising one-fifth of the island's sugarcane fields was set on fire and scores of slaves were killed, executed or deported. The news of the revolt took hours to reach the authorities in Bridgetown, so the following year the governor proposed that a chain of signal stations be built to aid communication. The network relayed messages by flags, to which watchful messengers responded by despatching the news to headquarters in Bridgetown. Following the abolition of slavery, the signal stations' crews passed the time by monitoring approaching cargo ships and announcing school times. An audio tape plays as you browse through displays of clay pipe fragments and musket balls. Climb the polished wooden staircase to the lookout at the top and imagine life before the telephone.

DID YOU KNOW?

Bay Rum is not a drink but an essential oil extracted from the bay tree. It is ideal for tensed muscles.

To the Island's Northern Tip

This drive covers the northern tip of the island, from the parish of St. Peter up to St. Lucy.

Head north on the coastal road out of Speightstown, keeping the sea to your left. Pass the entrance to Almond Beach Village and Port St. Charles Marina and turn right up a hill. Carry on over the intersection and look out for All Saints Church.

Flanked by sugarcane fields, All Saints Church, built in 1649, is the resting place of William Arnold, the first English settler. His grave is clearly marked.

Carry on to a T-junction, turn right and follow signs to the Barbados Wildlife Reserve (➤ 14).

Farley Hill National Park (➤ 37) appears first, to your left. Park inside and walk round the ruins. Leave the car where it is and cross the road to the Barbados Wildlife Reserve. After seeing the animals, birds and reptiles, have a drink or snack in the café before exploring nearby Grenade Hall Forest and Signal Station (➤ 38).

Leave Farley Hill and turn right towards the sails of the Morgan Lewis Sugar Mill (➤ 41), passing through wonderful scenery with views of the coast. Visit the mill before heading further north to the Animal Flower Cave (➤ 37).

At stunning North Point take tea and photos until it's time to head back on the coastal road to Speightstown.

Distance
Approx 16 miles (10km)

Time
Half a day with lunch, to a full day

Start/End Point
Speightstown
✠ 24A4

Lunch
Barbados Wildlife Reserve ($) or Animal Flower Cave ($)

❓ If you plan to walk the forest nature trail, wear stout shoes and be careful on the mossy paths. You can swim in the Animal Flower Cave

Waves crash on North Point, the island's northernmost tip

Arbib Nature & Heritage Trail

Distance
5 miles (7.5km); alternative
3.5 miles (5.5km) trail

Time
2 or 3½ hours, depending on
stops

Start/End Point
Speightstown
✚ 24A4

Lunch
Various places in
Speightstown ($–$$)

❓ Walks must be pre-
booked. ☎ 234 9010
Wear proper walking
shoes, a sun hat,
sunscreen and take
drinking water

*Hiking through sugarcane
fields on the Arbib Trail*

The Arbib Nature and Heritage Trail—run by the Barbados National Trust—won the Caribbean ecotourism award, beating entrants from 20 other islands. There are two trails of varying length: the longer "Whim Adventure" trail cuts through the Whim Gully, one of many gullies of limestone and coral that lead to the sea and drain the island's rainfall.

The trail begins from Speightstown and passes villages, sugarcane plantations and cottonfields. As you go, the guide stops to point out herbs and other plants that have medicinal uses, such as the castor-oil plant. You will weave through mango, banana and grapefruit trees, dog's dumpling, breadfruit, the bearded fig and a pumpkin patch.

In the interior villages you'll see Barbadian chattel houses, some with their own kitchen gardens. The chattel is built perfectly symmetrically with a door in the center and windows either side. Traditionally the roof is made of shingle, with a steep pitch to allow rain to run off easily. These tiny buildings withstand hurricanes pretty well, too. As the owner prospered he built more units, marked by another steep roof.

As the walk nears the coast the houses become grander. You can rest near the cannon at the remains of 18th-century Dover Fort, which overlooks the waterfront apartments of Port St. Charles, before heading back to Speightstown. Stroll back along the sandy beach that cuts in front of the Almond Beach Village before joining your guide for a drink at the rum shop at Speightstown harborside.

MORGAN LEWIS SUGAR MILL ✪✪

At one time Barbados had many wind-driven mills. They were introduced by the Dutch planters from Brazil when they brought sugarcane to the island in the 1600s, flattening the forests to make way for vast plantations worked by slaves from Africa. The mills crushed the sugarcane to extract the juice, which would then go through a process of boiling and cooling before finally ending as sugar for export. Built around 1776, the restored Morgan Lewis Sugar Mill is the largest complete windmill in the Caribbean. It is set within a working farm and occupies a gorgeous position, flanked by a row of mahogany trees. Inside is the grinding machinery, made by a firm in Derby, England. Although not as vital as tourism, the sugar industry is still important to Barbados.

SIX MEN'S BAY ✪

At the coastal village of Six Men's Bay wooden fishing boats, waiting to be treated or repaired, are pulled up onto the grass beyond the shoreline. Nets and floats lie scattered about, as do chunks of mahogany used by boatbuilders to make the keels. If you're lucky, you might see work being carried out. Usually the boatbuilders don't mind if you stop to chat or ask questions. Pretty wooden houses line one side of the road while the sea laps the sands opposite, making this a refreshing place to rest before reaching Speightstown.

SPEIGHTSTOWN (▶ 21, TOP TEN)

🔲 24B4
✉ Near Cherry Tree Hill, St. Andrew
☎ 422 7429
🕐 Mon–Sat 9–5
🚌 Not recommended, as a long way from the nearest bus stop
♿ Few
💵 Moderate
❓ See grinding of sugar cane (check local newspaper or phone for times)

🔲 24A4
✉ Near Speightstown
🍴 Rum shops and restaurants in Speightstown ($–$$)
🚌 Speightstown bus from Bridgetown
♿ None

Above: *Morgan Lewis Sugar Mill*

What to See on the East Coast

ANDROMEDA BOTANIC GARDENS (➤ 12–13, TOP TEN)

BATHSHEBA (➤ 15, TOP TEN)

CHALKY MOUNT VILLAGE (➤ 17, TOP TEN)

THE CRANE   ✪✪

Try and visit this historic hotel on a Sunday morning so you can enjoy the brunch and foot-tapping live gospel by local singers. It takes place in the clifftop terrace restaurant overlooking the cliffs and the Atlantic. To one side is the hotel pool: the majestic white colonnades surrounding a circle of blue and backed by the ocean have been photographed by dozens of fashion magazines. To the other side, sheer cliffs drop to the famous pink sands of Crane Beach.

Opened in 1887 on the site of an 18th-century mansion and lit by oil lamps, The Crane was the first resort hotel on Barbados. At that time, ladies bathed discreetly in a specially built area called "the horse." The original steps cut into the cliff, leading to "the horse," remain. As for the name of the hotel, it came about when there was a small commercial port here and a crane was used to raise and lower cargo on and off the trading ships that docked.

Opposite: Breakers crash onto the rocks by picturesque Crane Beach

🚫 25D2
✉ Crane, St. Philip
☎ 423 6220
🕐 Brunch Sun 9.30am; singing Sun 10–11am; Bajan buffet Sun 12.30–3
🍴 Restaurant ($$–$$$) noted for its seafood, especially oysters
🚌 From Bridgetown catch the Sam Lord bus
♿ Few
💵 Moderate

Fewer tourists find the Bathsheba coastline

✛ 25D2
✉ St. Philip
🍴 Cafés and restaurants
  ($–$$$) on way
🚌 To Crane Beach or Sam
  Lord's Castle
♿ None
💵 Free

✛ 25D2
✉ Long Bay, St. Philip
☎ 423 7350
🕐 Daily, morning to sunset
🍴 Cafés and restaurants
  ($–$$$) on the resort
🚌 From Bridgetown take
  the Sam Lord bus
♿ Few
💵 Moderate; includes
  access to the beach

RAGGED POINT ❂❂

An old lighthouse marks Ragged Point, the most easterly point of the island. It is a wonderfully exposed, tranquil spot. Though the lighthouse is no longer open to the public, its beams still warn sailors to keep their ships away from the limestone cliffs and Cobbler's Reef. Slightly to the north of the lighthouse is tiny, uninhabited Culpepper Island, Barbados's only "colony".

SAM LORD'S CASTLE ❂❂❂

If ever Barbados had an extravagant rascal it was the infamous Sam Lord, who reputedly kept his heiress wife in a cellar. His turreted seat, Sam Lord's Castle, is a former plantation house turned pricey, all-inclusive 71-acre (29-ha) resort. According to legend, Lord hung lamps in trees on the clifftop to lure cargo ships onto the treacherous rocks. Once they were wrecked, Lord seized the treasure. Some say he had tunnels built from the castle to the beach and that he brought the treasure back himself. Rumor has it that the treasure is still buried somewhere in the castle grounds. Lord died heavily in debt and, as with all juicy stories, it is said his ghost paces the corridors and chambers. The castle, built in 1820 by craftsmen from England who created a superb interior from Barbados mahogany, is also noted for its ceilings and Lord's four-poster bed. Unless you're a guest you pay an admission fee to roam the terraced gardens and see inside, which is laid out for viewing with ropes sectioning off the interesting areas. Towards the cliff a stone walkway juts over the ocean and a sandy, palm-strewn stretch known as Long Bay. There is a good view of the castle from here.

Above: *The former castle of the notorious Sam Lord is claimed to be haunted*

SUNBURY PLANTATION HOUSE (➤ 22, TOP TEN)

Along the East Coast Road

The East Coast Road (also called the Ermie Bourne Highway) runs through the parishes of St. Andrew and St. Joseph between the Atlantic Ocean and the Scotland District. Opened in 1966 by Queen Elizabeth II, the road slithers along the route of the old railway from Bridgetown to Belleplaine and passes three of our Top Ten attractions.

Have your hotel prepare a picnic lunch beforehand so you can stop and spend an hour sitting on the sands. Remember, it is too dangerous for swimming, but at low tide you can potter around the rock pools.

Start from Bathsheba (➤ 15). Spend a while at Andromeda Botanic Gardens (➤ 12–13) and Bathsheba village before heading north, keeping the ocean to your right.

Worn, wooden chattel houses face deserted beaches scattered with rock formations and giant boulders. Next comes Cattlewash. The road here is not busy, so you can stop at intervals to take photographs. The Scotland District on your left, so called because it reminded British settlers of the Scottish Highlands, is a rugged area of steep lanes with sheep and cattle grazing on the hillsides. Many potters exploit the clay deposits in this area (➤ 17).

Drive on a little farther to reach a peaceful resting spot, Barclays Park, a picnic area popular with locals on public holidays. On weekdays, you might be the only visitor. The park was a gift from Barclays Bank in 1966, the year of independence.

This short drive ends at the village of Belleplaine, where the railroad once terminated.

Distance
4 miles (6.5km)

Time
Half a day with lunch and stops

Start Point
Bathsheba
✚ 25C3

End Point
Belleplaine
✚ 24B4

Lunch
Take a picnic or have a Bajan buffet at Edgewater Inn ($)
✉ Bathsheba beach
☎ 433 9900
❓ The drive can be done in reverse and linked with part of the drive to the Island's Northern tip (➤ 39).

On the east side of the island the Scotland District rambles to the Atlantic Coast

In the Know

If you only have a short time to visit Barbados, or would like to get a real flavor of the island, here are some ideas:

10
Ways to Be a Local

- **Chill** man.
- Keep **beachwear** strictly for the beach.
- Take your **rum punch** neat.
- Get into the **reggae** beat.
- Hit the beach **before the crowds** and watch the sun rise.
- Rent a **mobile phone** to pose.
- Learn the uses of **Barbados's flora.**
- Go to **church** on Sunday.
- Learn the **Bajan dialect.**
- Know the history of **sugarcane and slavery.**

10
Good Places to Have Lunch

Brown Sugar ($$–$$$)
St. Michael ☎ 426 7684. Planter's Buffet Sun–Fri.
Bubba's Sports Bar ($)
Rodeley, Christ Church ☎ 435 8731. Local dishes, seafood and international kids' meals.
Cobbler's Cove ($$$)
Cobbler's Cove, St. Peter ☎ 422 2291. Relais et Chateaux restaurant within Cobbler's Cove Hotel. Reservations required.
Edgewater Inn ($)
Bathsheba, St. Joseph ☎ 433 9900. Bajan buffet and views over the ocean. (➤ 15).
Hibiscus Café ($–$$)
Andromeda Botanic

Gardens ☎ 433 9261 or 433 9384. Light meals, snacks or a picnic lunch to eat in the gardens (➤ 12–13).
Patisserie Flindt ($), Holetown, St. James

☎ 432 2626. Pastries, puddings and ice cream.
Round House Inn & Bar ($)
Bathsheba ☎ 433 9678. Take in the great views with your lunch.

Opa's Greek Restaurant ($$), Hastings, Christ Church ☎ 435 1234. Family-run; authentic moussaka and souvlaki, with views of the ocean.
Ship Inn—Captain's Carvery ($), St. Lawrence Gap, Christ Church ☎ 435 6961. Tasty Bajan buffet.
Sugar Sugar Beach Bar ($$–$$$), Mullins Bay, St. Peter ☎ 422 1878. Light lunches overlooking the beach.

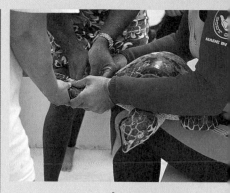

10
Top Activities

- Watch a game of **cricket.**
- **Bet on the horses** at the historic Garrison Savannah.
- **Snorkel** with the turtles.
- **Dive** the coral reefs and wrecks (▶ 59).
- Go on a 4WD **adventure safari.**
- Take a **Sunday stroll** with the Barbados National Trust (▶ 9).
- Hop aboard a yacht and go **sailing.**
- Try your swing at one of the **golf** courses (▶ 84).
- Go **horse riding**
- Learn to **windsurf.**

Above: *tagging a hawksbill turtle*

5
Ways to Help the Environment

- Help to keep the **beaches clean.**
- **Don't feed the fish** or other wildlife, as it alters their natural feeding habits.
- **Learn about plants and fruits** on the Arbib Nature and Heritage Trail (▶ 40).
- Discover how to **protect the world's rainforests** at the Grenade Hall Forest (▶ 38).

- **Seen a hatching?** Contact the Barbados Turtle Project. 24-hr hotline ☎ 230 0142.

5
Ways to Let Your Hair Down

- **Sing** at a karaoke.
- Wear **swimming gear only** to a Harbour Lights beach party (▶ 82).
- **Dance** at the Reggae Lounge in St. Lawrence Gap.
- See live **limbo dancing.**
- Try the **rum.**

5
Best Viewpoints

- North Point (▶ 39).
- Bathsheba (▶ 15).
- Ragged Point (▶ 44).
- Silver Sands (▶ 56).
- Mullins Bay (▶ 65).

Left: *Close of day on the terrace of Cobbler's Cove*
Far left: *Windsurfers ride the waves at the Silver Sands Beach*

What to See on the South Coast

24A1
St. Michael
429 2113
Tours: Mon–Fri 8–4.
Closed Wed
Rachel Pringle Bar for
beer tasting, cafés and
restaurants ($–$$$) in
Bridgetown
From Bridgetown
None   Inexpensive

24A1
Historic Garrison, St.
Michael
228 0149
Tue–Sat 10–5
Cafés and restaurants
($–$$$) in Bridgetown
From Bridgetown
None
Inexpensive
Guided tours available,
but must be booked;
public lectures

BANKS (BARBADOS) BREWERIES ★

Wherever you go on the island you'll see black, red and white billboards announcing that, apart from rum, the only thing to drink on Barbados is Banks beer. During a tour of the breweries, just outside Bridgetown, you can see it being brewed, visit the old brew house and have a tasting. Notice that the copper kettles, used for the brewing process for 30 years, have been replaced by modern steel vats that can each hold 3,080gal (14,000L) of beer. Even more astounding is the bottling hall, where 250,000 bottles of Banks are capped each day.

BARBADOS GALLERY OF ART ★

A collection of around 300 oil paintings, watercolors, drawings and sculptures gathered over the past decade belong to the Barbados Gallery of Art, the island's museum of fine art. Works are by artists from not only the Caribbean but the United States and South America. There are two exhibition galleries and the collection rotates six times a year. Pieces are also borrowed from private collections so it's worth making return visits.

A typical rum shop at St Lawrence Gap

GRAEME HALL BIRD SANCTUARY (▶ 9)

HERITAGE PARK AND FOURSQUARE RUM DISTILLERY ✪✪✪

Voted by a newspaper in the United States as "one of the most modern rum distilleries in the world," the Heritage Park and Foursquare Rum Distillery comes complete with its own integrated recycling plant. If that alone isn't a sufficient draw, there is plenty more to see at this attraction, which covers 7 acres (3ha) of a once sprawling sugar plantation and includes one of the island's oldest sugar factories. In an outdoor museum filled with machinery, you can see how rum was made in the early days, or you can go underground at the furnace and feel what it was like to be a boiler worker. Nowadays, the distillery is known for its top-selling ESAF White Rum, Orland Brigand and Doorly's Rum, which, naturally, you are given the opportunity to taste.

Capitalizing on the popularity of the Heritage Park, there are exhibitions of paintings by local artists in the on-site art galleries. There are also demonstrations of glass blowing and screen printing, and regular lunch and dinner cultural shows in the Cane Pit Amphitheatre.

➕ 25C2
✉ Foursquare, St. Philip
☎ 420 1977
🕐 Mon–Fri 8–5
🍴 Sugar Cane Café ($–$$) on site
🚌 From Bridgetown take the St. Patrick bus
♿ Good
💲 Moderate; includes access to the beach
❓ 40-minute tour available for cruise parties only who book in advance

➕ 24A4
✉ Spring Garden Highway
☎ 425 9066
🕐 Daily 8–4.30
🍴 Lunch tours Tue–Thu ($)
🚌 From Bridgetown, take the Deacon road bus
♿ Good
🥤 Moderate

MOUNT GAY RUM DISTILLERY ●●●

For the rundown on rum and a sip of the neat stuff, visit the Mount Gay Rum Distillery, reputedly the home of the world's oldest rum. (This is actually the blending and bottling factory; the distillery is in St. Lucy, in the north.) Step in to a traditional-style chattel house and learn about the history of rum since 1703, right up to how it's aged, blended and bottled today. If you book a special luncheon tour with one of the sightseeing operators, or through your resort/hotel rep, then transport, a Bajan buffet and a free miniature bottle of rum are included. Of course, you can taste the rum in comfort at the on-site shop. Note how the bottles line wooden shelves behind the bar as they do in rum shops all over the island.

OISTINS

✪✪✪

By day, Oistins is a busy fishing village that supplies fresh fish and shellfish to the whole of the island. Boats are forever landing catches and those that aren't are pulled up on the grassy sand dunes for repair or paintwork. Walk among the lobster pots and nets, then watch the fishmongers gutting and packing the fish in ice at the fish terminal. You can get a cheap bite to eat here at lunchtimes, but the real draw is the enormously popular Friday night Fish Fry, when stallholders fry flying fish, dolphin, shark, barracuda and snapper after sunset. Order your fish with rice or a helping of macaroni cheese pie and a bottle of Banks beer. There's music, long lines at the counters and dancing by the tables. Saturday nights are also popular, but even better is the Oistins Fish Festival, which runs over the Easter weekend.

✚ 24B1
✉ Christ Church
🍴 Excellent freshly fried fish at stalls ($)
🚌 From Bridgetown
♿ Few

Left: *Oak barrels of ageing rum line the cellars of the Mount Gay Rum Distillery*
Inset: *sampling the delights of the island's tipple on the distillery tour*
Below: *frying fish*

Food & Drink

Barbadian fare is built on dishes of African origin, spiced up for the Caribbean, with English-inspired, crust-free cucumber sandwiches thrown in for good measure.

Above: *Flying fish, which is skinned, de-boned and fried to create the national dish*

Below: *A mouth-watering barbecue banquet of fish steaks and pork sausages*

National Dishes

The premier national dish is flying fish, a silvery-blue, sardine-like fish that actually flaps its fins to enable it to glide above the surface of the sea. Once de-boned, the fish is rolled in breadcrumbs and Bajan seasoning, then deep fried. Other catches of the day are barracuda, dolphin (sometimes listed on the menu as *mahi mahi*), tuna, kingfish and snapper. Lobster and shrimps harvested in Guyana are grilled and drizzled with oil or smothered in sauces.

Fish is blended into a chowder or battered as fishcakes and served with the island's own hot pepper sauce. Take care with the ubiquitous bottle of Bajan sauce placed on the table. One dash is enough, three is explosive. For real home food, seek out a cook shop and watch all parts of a chicken, pig or black-bellied sheep go in a big pot for simmering. A pudding and souse is actually sausage, sweet potato and boiled pig's head and feet served with cucumber and pepper pickle.

Another national dish is *cou-cou*, made from cornmeal and okra pudding and similar to the African dish *foo-foo*. Primarily, the local diet is rich in starch, derived from sweet potatoes, yams and fried plantains (like a banana but must

be cooked before eating). Breadfruit was introduced to the island by Captain Bligh of *Mutiny on the Bounty* fame, and pumpkins are made into a delicious soup. Rice mixed with peas is a popular side dish, as is macaroni cheese pie. Look out for set-priced Bajan buffets where you help yourself to a dozen typical dishes. For fast food, Bajans prefer chicken, or a roti filled with meat or fish curry. For dessert, try paw paw, mango, passion fruit, cherries, papaya, or coconut sweet pie and butter pudding.

Alcoholic Drinks

A rum shop is a small bar and local gathering haunt where Bajans discuss cricket and politics and play dominoes or the old African game called *warri*. They order a plate of fish and a shot of rum, which comes dark or as clear as pure vodka. The connoisseur usually selects a five-year-old blend. Drink it neat, with crushed ice, with cola or shaken into a cocktail. Hotels and bars concoct their own mindblowers. Daiquiri is a delicious blend of mango or banana pulp, rum, lime juice, ice and sugar. Gin and coconut water also goes down well. Banks beer is for sale everywhere and is best drunk ice-cold from the bottle.

Above: *Refreshing and exceedingly popular— rum punch dressed with fresh fruit*

Non-alcoholic Drinks

English afternoon tea served complete with a tier of cakes, cream scones and cucumber sandwiches is a west coast tradition. Chilled ginger beer is as refreshing as a fresh coconut, its top hacked off and a straw plunged into the milk. *Sorrel* is a Christmas tipple, made from plant leaves infused in hot water and spices. Bars sell fruit punches and real juices, lemonade actually made from lemons and internationally known brands of cola and canned drinks.

Below: *Afternoon tea served on the terrace at the Royal Pavilion Hotel on the west coast*

Tasty Snacks

There are plenty of snack items on Barbados to keep you munching indulgently between meals. Try cashew nuts, tamarind balls, jam puffs or nachos with cheese. You should also taste the freshest bananas sold by the roadside and a delicious flying fish sandwich known as a *cutter*.

A Sunday Drive

One Sunday morning, skip breakfast and head along the south coast to hear gospel singing at The Crane hotel (➤ 43). En route you'll see Bajan women in dresses, hats and white gloves attending church. Some men wear their Sunday best suits. Quietly and unobtrusively, stop outside any church and listen to the hymns.

Start from Oistins (➤ 51) on the Maxwell main road and head east, following the signs to the airport. You'll drive through villages with painted houses and cane fields. Follow the signs to Crane Beach.

Arrive at The Crane hotel at 9.30am in time for Sunday brunch at 10.30 and enjoy the entertainment. Afterwards, walk down to Crane Bay for swimming, sunbathing or body boarding.

Drive out of Crane Beach and head northwards, passing Belair Golf Course, until you reach Sam Lord's Castle (➤ 44).

Above: *A gospel singer from The Crane hotel*
Opposite: *Crane Beach*

An admission fee allows you to look round the castle, grounds and beach.

Finish up at Ragged Point (➤ 44) for a brief walk and lunch.

On the drive back you can take a right detour to Sunbury Plantation House (➤ 22) for afternoon tea before heading back towards Oistins.

If the day is still young, take a left detour through small communities to reach Silver Sands beach (➤ 56).

Watch the windsurfers flip 360 degrees above the waves. Look out for the South Point Lighthouse, made in England out of cast iron and shipped in pieces to the island. It was reassembled and working by 1852.

Alternatively, head straight back along the coastal road to Oistins fishing village for the perfect finale—a succulent Fish Fry in the open.

Distance
Approx 7 miles (12km)

Time
Half a day with lunch and stops

Start Point
Oistins
✚ 24B1

End Point
Ragged Point
✚ 25D2

Brunch
Brunch at The Crane hotel ($$)
✉ St. Philip
☎ 423 6220

The Silver Rock Hotel has a swimming pool at the water's edge

+ 24B1
⊠ South coast, east of Bridgetown
🍴 Bars and restaurants ($–$$)—some with live music
🚌 Any south coast bus from Bridgetown
♿ None

+ 25C1
⊠ Silver Sands, Christ Church
☎ 428 2866
🍴 Snacks ($) nearby and at Silver Rock Hotel ($$)
♿ None

+ 24B1
⊠ Wildey, St. Michael
☎ 426 2421
🕐 Jan–Apr Wed 2.30–5.30
🍴 Plenty on south coast
♿ None
🎫 Free

ST. LAWRENCE GAP ✪

Moving westwards along the south coast, the closer you get to Bridgetown the livelier it becomes. St. Lawrence Gap is where the party people go, although regulars say it's not as friendly and easy-going as it used to be. Sports bars with video screens, live blues, Happy Hours and karaoke, souvenir shells and painted maracas are what it's all about. There's a string of good restaurants and, in between the hotels and apartment blocks, crescents of sandy beach and safe swimming. You can learn to dive, water-ski or just hang on to a banana boat.

SILVER SANDS ✪

Silver Sands beach at the southern tip of the island is a Mecca for professional windsurfers. The all-inclusive Silver Rock Resort, actually overlooking the tip, offers a whole range of thrills for outdoor enthusiasts. As well as windsurfing you can try boogie boarding, hiking and wilderness and adventure diving. The star of the windsurfing scene is local champion Brian Talma, who offers lessons to intermediate windsurfers.

WILDEY HOUSE ✪✪

Wildey House, a Georgian hilltop mansion set in beautiful grounds, is the headquarters of the Barbados National Trust. Historic photographs of Barbados and exquisite silver are displayed among antique furniture in carefully dressed rooms. The Trust is important to the island because it enables its architecture, sometimes dating back more than 350 years, to be preserved and maintained. Since 1961 the Trust has taken on the care of eight properties, including a wooded gully (➤ 72), the largest sugar mill in the Caribbean (➤ 41) and a botanic garden (➤ 12–13). It has also helped to create an underwater park (➤ 60) on the west coast and has identified Bush Hill (➤ 19) as the house in which George Washington, President of the United States, stayed in 1751.

A Submarine Cruise

There are few places in the world where you can board a real submarine and submerge for an undersea exploration. Complete with Captain Nemo-style sounds and live dialogue between the crew and the surface, the Atlantis Submarine trip is pricey, but shouldn't be missed.

First, you board the *Ocean Crest* catamaran and sail out of Bridgetown's harbor to reach the submarine. Look out for visiting cruise ships and partygoers on the *Jolly Roger* pirate ship. Safety instructions are given before you are invited to board.

In 1994 Atlantis became the world's first passenger submarine fleet and is still going down well. Stretching 66ft (20m) and weighing 80 tonnes, the *Atlantis III* sinks slowly to 151ft (46m). It then cruises gently above the seabed off the west coast at 1½ knots. You sit with the other passengers on benches, facing outwards through large portholes.

The seabed is white, like laid snow. A wreck appears, the fish darting in and out of its gaps. Next comes a garden of brain coral, ferns and sponges. If you're lucky, a turtle might glide gracefully by. For definite, you'll see thousands of fish, from stingrays to barracudas and shoals of colorful species. If you've ever wanted to scuba dive but lacked the courage, this is the next best thing.

Even more spectacular is Atlantis By Night, a cruise taken when the coral is at its most striking and nocturnal predators come out to feed. The submarine's lights illuminate the coral and fish and you'll see the wreck of the *Lord Willoughby*. Whichever trip you take, at the end you're given a certificate to prove that you took the plunge.

Time
1 hour

Start/End point
Atlantis Submarines
✠ 24A1
✉ The Shallow Draught, Bridgetown
☎ 436 8929
🚌 Nearest bus station is Bridgetown; take a taxi to the harbor
✋ Expensive
❓ Book through Atlantis Submarines, a tour operator, or your hotel or resort rep.

Lunch
Sublime Café ($)
✉ On site

The Atlantis III *submarine prepares to dive to the ocean floor*

What to See on the West Coast

BARBADOS POLO CLUB ✪✪

✚ 24A2
✉ Holders Hill, St. James
☎ 427 0022
♿ None
🎫 Free, but priced tickets for international matches

Polo on the island dates back to the 1900s and was introduced by the British cavalry who, having tired of playing against each other, roped in the locals. The Barbados Polo Club was established at what is now the historic Garrison in Bridgetown in 1929 and moved in the 1960s to its current location on Holder's Hill in St. James with its wide grassland and towering trees. Recently, three new polo fields have been developed. Each year, October to the end of May, the season's intinerary includes fixtures against international teams, bolstered by Bajan hospitality. These matches are well attended by tourists, many of whom regard Barbados polo as one of the most vibrating sports on the island. Afternoon tea and those crustless cucumber sandwiches are served in style in the atmospheric wooden clubhouse after the game.

Below: *Polo is a favorite sport on the Island*

EARTHWORKS POTTERY ✪✪

✚ 24B2
✉ St. James
☎ 425 0223
🕐 Mon–Fri 9–5 (except public hols), Sat 9–1
🍴 The Lunch Club ($–$$), ☎ 425 2890
🚌 From Bridgetown, take Hillaby or Shop Hill bus
♿ Few
🎫 Free

Earthworks Pottery is another showcase for Barbadian art crafted from local clay. Founded in 1983 as a small art studio making individual pieces, the pottery has expanded and now produces a range of trinket bowls, carvings, custom-made tiles and glassware—and yes—all major credit cards are accepted. It's a bright and cheerful place where practically everything except the trees and grass are painted. After touring the pottery and, during working hours, watching the artists, you can dine on light meals on the veranda next to a bamboo patch.

Diving from Barbados

Barbados is as beautiful below the waves as above, and the best places to scuba dive are the west and southwest coasts. The west in particular is sheltered, with good visibility and warm temperatures. Underneath is a coral wonderland of 6.5-ft (2-m) sponges, sea fans and black corals. Fish include barracudas, jacks, mackerel and thousands of other brightly colored tropical fish. Spot rare species such as batfish, frogfish and sea horses. There are three types of turtle, the hawksbill, leatherback and green. Most common is the hawksbill, seen frequently by divers and snorkelers. Barbados has its own diving association, the Professional Association of Dive Operators, PADO, and a number of operators offer lessons at all levels (➤ 85). Here's a taster of what lurks beneath.

Bridgetown's Carlisle Bay is a natural harbor, its seabed scattered with whisky and rum bottles thrown over by sailors of old. Cannon and anchors are dotted about. Three shipwrecks can be seen on one dive.

From **Folkestone Underwater Park** (➤ 60) you travel by boat to a number of diving spots on Dottins Reef. See massive sea fans, soft corals, sea lilies, barracudas and turtles. **SS** *Stavronikita* is the largest and most-talked-about wreck on the island. Measuring 121yds (111m) long, the Greek cargo ship caught fire off Barbados in 1976. Purposely sunk, she now sits bolt upright on the seabed, her masts reaching to within 20ft (6m) of the surface.

> ## DID YOU KNOW?
> Barbados is made from coral, the accumulated skeletons of millions of dead sea creatures. Apart from some exposed ridges to the north, most of the island is coated with a cap of limestone up to 600,000 years old. Chunks of grooved coral are sometimes washed up and large finds are displayed as ornaments in some hotels.

Snuba
A shallow water diving system with no tanks, just an airline connected to a surface tank. It's easy and no certification is needed (☎ 233 7626/246 2088).

Coral gardens and a dazzling array of fish beckon divers of all abilities

24A3
Porters, St. James
422 5555
Call for details
Afternoon tea daily 3.30–5
From Bridgetown or Speightstown
Good

24A3
Folkestone, St. James
422 2314
Park open daily, museum Mon–Fri 9–5
Beach bars and cafés/picnic area
From Speightstown, Holetown, Bridgetown
Few   Park free, museum inexpensive

FAIRMONT GLITTER BAY AND ROYAL PAVILION ESTATE ✪✪

The west coast has many pseudonyms, "Platinum Coast," "Gold Coast" and even "Millionaires Row," maybe because its sands are silvery or gold, and the hotels ultra-glamorous and extremely expensive. Commanding an historic estate is the Fairmont Glitter Bay Hotel, twinned with the Royal Pavilion, where writers meet their publishers and where Sir Edward Cunard, one of the world's greatest shipping magnates, lived. His original turreted beach house has been turned into exclusive, expensive suites. Renowned South American-born landscape architect Fernando Tabora created the tropical gardens here. There is a weekly, guided botanic tour of the courtyards, beds and lily ponds on Tuesdays at 10am. You follow the head gardener through more than 400 coconut trees. If you're smartly dressed, you can take afternoon tea in the Palm Terrace restaurant of the Royal Pavilion over-looking the sea. In traditional 1930s manner, a white pot of Earl Grey, Darjeeling, peppermint or camomile tea is brought to your table, accompanied by a tiered stand of chocolate brownies, pastries, jam turnovers and crustless sandwiches.

> ### DID YOU KNOW?
> The grapefruit originated from Barbados in the late 1700s.

A lily pond features on the botanical tour of the Fairmont Glitter Bay hotel gardens

FOLKESTONE UNDERWATER PARK ✪

Not solely of interest to scuba divers, the park tells the story of the marine life of the island through its museum. Here you'll learn interesting snippets: for example, did you know the sex of a sea turtle is determined by the temper-ature of the sand the eggs are laid in? Then go snorkeling in the sea to see fish, sponges and coral. Nearby, operators will take you out to Dottins Reef wrecks and more reefs in glass-bottomed boats.

The Platinum Coast

This drive takes you along the polished west coast, past the most expensive restaurants and hotels on the island, parish churches and golf courses.

Start at the southern end of the coastal road, at the roundabout with the ABC Highway. Head north, following signs to west coast/ Speightstown, keeping the Caribbean Sea close to your left.

If you have time, take a look at the exterior of the University of the West Indies, which overlooks Bridgetown. The campus was opened in 1962.

Continue north and make a short stop at Paynes Bay for a cool drink on the beach and even a swim. Back on the road, on your right, is the Sandy Lane 18–hole championship golf course.

The revamped Sandy Lane estate is one of the most luxurious and expensive places to park your suitcase. Originally, the property was built by a rich Anglo-American, Ronald Tree, as a holiday retreat for his friends. No expense was spared and after an opening involving much pomp and ceremony in 1961, the likes of Mick Jagger, Tom Jones and Jacqueline Kennedy Onassis stayed.

Continue northwards to Holetown (► 66), the next major attraction.

Here you can stop for lunch, sightseeing and shopping.

Head north again along the coast. You can drive directly to Speightstown (► 21), past a string of luxury hotels, to explore the island's second biggest town.

Check out the ice cream and pastries at Patisserie Flindt, or stop at intervals along the way.

To reach the beach, walk through alleyways of beachfront villas and wooden chattel houses. Mullins Bay (► 65) is an obvious choice.

Distance
5.5 miles (9km)

Time
Half a day with stops

Start Point
Roundabout near the University of the West Indies
✚ 24A2

End Point
Speightstown
✚ 24A4

Lunch
Numerous places along the coast ($$–$$$)
Patisserie Flindt ($)
✉ Holetown, St James
☎ 432 2626

Golfers flock to the Sandy Lane golf course, overlooking the sea

Best Beaches

Barbados has around 69 miles (112km) of coastline and public beaches. The west is calm enough for swimming, snorkeling and waterskiing; the south is for windsurfing; and the east is the domain of experienced surfers and body boarders only, and for spectacular photography.

West Coast

Fitts Village offers good snorkeling and is within reach of the Malibu Beach Club, which has its own beach, offering watersports and beach volleyball. A visitor center shows you how Malibu rum is made.

Paynes Bay has palm trees growing out of the sand and hawkers selling sarongs, shirts, Reggae hats, sunglasses, coconuts and sunloungers.

Mullins Beach is a busy favorite where you can do anything, from snorkeling to whizzing around on a jet ski. Sit in a deck chair and have your hair braided and beaded, sunbathe, or perch on a stool at the bamboo bar and sip a cocktail.

Below: Chilled cocktails on sale from the bamboo bar at Mullins Beach

Opposite: The Caribbean Sea gently laps the soft sands of the west coast

South Coast

Accra Beach is usually packed with well-toned people sunbathing, strutting around or body surfing. It's great for posing and people-watching.

Sandy Beach is ideal for families with children as it is protected by a reef that creates a shallow lagoon calm enough for swimming and snorkeling. You can also get to grips with windsurfing before progressing to Silver Sands.

Breezy **Silver Sands** (► 56) at the southern tip of the island is home to windsurfing experts, though intermediate windsurfers can receive lessons. It is a refreshing place with much watersport activity.

East Coast

Crane Bay is beloved for its high cliffs plunging down to pink-tinged sands and a white-tipped ocean, apparently perfect for surfing.

At **Bottom Bay**, north of Sam Lord's Castle (► 44), admire the views then head down the cliff steps and weave through the palms that decorate the white sands.

Bathsheba (► 15) is pounded by the Atlantic Ocean and scattered with strange boulders. Breathtaking it is, though the current makes it too dangerous for swimming.

A Beach Walk

An easy-going stroll punctuated by swimming and sunning, and ending with a fantastic sunset.

From Speightstown (► 21), follow the lane leading to the beach and turn left into the curve of a cove, overlooked by the Cobbler's Cove Hotel.

Here early evening strollers may have witnessed the mass exodus of turtle hatchlings, heading from their nests to the sea. Just before Cobbler's Cove is a river outlet where cheerful vendors sell Hawaiian-style shirts made from a single piece of fabric. If you buy a sarong, you'll be shown half a dozen different ways to wear it.

Wander along the beach littered with fragments of bone-white coral, passing sunbathers on loungers outside the King's Beach Hotel.

Notice the three coconut palms bending almost horizontally to the sea. On Barbados everything from this tree is used. The fruit makes a coconut drink, the flesh is scraped and used in baking scones (biscuits), the husk for souvenirs, the trunk for building houses and the palm fronds for weaving baskets.

Pass wooden beach shacks where women sit outside and scrape the scales off freshly caught fish. You'll probably see the square fishing baskets that are left on the seabed for days until the fish swim in and become trapped. Often there is a fisherman at the shoreline casting out his fishing net.

Rounding the corner you'll see the full stretch of Mullins Bay, and a small market selling beachwear. This is a good place to sit at the beach bar and drink a piña colada before retracing your steps back along the beach. Alternatively, return along the coastal road, take the bus, or hitch a ride on a jet ski.

Above: *The three palms landmark is seen on a stroll to Mullins Beach*

Distance
0.62 miles (1km)

Time
Half to a full day with swimming and stops

Start Point
Speightstown beach
✚ 24A4

End Point
Mullins Bay
✚ 24A3

Lunch
Mannie's ($)
✉ Suga Suga beach bar, Mullin's Beach
☎ 419 4511

Opposite: *Rasta hats and sarongs make cheap and cheerful souvenirs*

HOLETOWN ✪✪✪

You can spend a full day in Holetown or, during February, a full week at the annual Holetown Festival. The festival coincides with the landing of the first British settlers to the island on February 17, 1627. Prior to this, Englishman Captain John Powell, sailing the *Olive Blossom* to Brazil, anchored off the small natural harbor and set foot at what he declared Jamestown. Later, the settlement was renamed "the Hole" after a tiny inlet where boats could harbor. Back in England, Powell reported his discovery to his employer, Sir William Courteen, an Anglo-Dutch merchant. Courteen responded by sending out an expedition of about 80 settlers and a group of African slaves captured from a Spanish galleon. Powell headed the mission, sailing the *William and John*. More white settlers followed, setting up home and establishing crops of cotton, ginger and tobacco. They soon found out how to tend and utilize the soil using methods taught to them by Arawak Indians brought over especially from Guyana. Commemorating the landing is the Holetown Monument on the forecourt of the town's police station, the former fort. The date, for some reason, mistakenly reads 1605.

Around the town are a few buildings dating from the 17th century. St. James was the first church, originally built of wood. Inside is the old font and a bell inscribed "God Bless King William, 1696." Modern day gems include the exceptional Patisserie Flindt (➤ 77), plus a cheerful chattel village of craftshops and an art gallery.

➕ 24A3
✉ St. James
🍴 Excellent cafés and bars ($–$$)
🚌 From Bridgetown, Speightstown, Bathsheba
♿ Few

> ### DID YOU KNOW?
>
> Royal Palms are so called because they stand straight and erect, unlike the bendy coconut palms. Two perfect rows of Royal Palms flank the driveway leading to the Fairmont Royal Pavilion Hotel (➤ 79).

Calypso music, costume and dance at the annual Holetown Festival

FRANK HUTSON SUGAR MUSEUM ◐◐

Yet another property run by the Barbados National Trust is the Sir Frank Hutson Sugar Museum. Its collection of old sugar objects and machinery portrays the story of what was once the most prized commodity on the island. The collection was started by Barbadian engineer Sir Frank Hutson and is a tribute to his passion. During the cane-grinding season, from February to May, you can step over to the boiling house at the Portvale Sugar Factory, one of a few factories still working on the island, for a dollop of molasses.

TYROL COT HERITAGE VILLAGE ◐◐◐

Just over 2.5 acres (1ha) of landscaped gardens encompass Tyrol Cot Heritage Village, said to be the birth-place of Barbadian democracy. Built in 1854, the house was home to the late Sir Grantley Adams, founder of the Barbados Labour Party, from 1929. He was first premier of Barbados and the only prime minister of the short-lived West Indies Federation. Adams was one of the 10 national heroes named by the present prime minister, who also declared Adams's birthdate (April 28, 1898) National Heroes Day and a public holiday. Adams's son, Tom, who became prime minister from 1976 to 1985, was born here. Restored by the Barbados National Trust, the house is built of coral stone blocks. Inside it still has the Adams's own Barbadian antique furniture. Within the 4-acre (1.5-ha) grounds is a craft village in the style of a traditional chattel house settlement. You can buy handmade souvenirs by local artists here. There are working blacksmiths and the replica of an 1820s thatched slave hut revealing the simple way slaves lived in the days of the great sugar plantations.

✚ 24A3
✉ St. James
☎ 432 0100
🕐 Mon–Sat 9–5 (except public hol)
🍴 Excellent cafés ($–$$) on the coast road
🚌 From Bridgetown take the Rock Hall bus
♿ Few
✋ Museum inexpensive, factory tour extra

✚ 24B2
✉ Codrington Hill, St. Michael
☎ 424 2074
🕐 Mon–Fri 9–5; shops close earlier sometimes
🍴 Snacks available from the shops
🚌 From Bridgetown, take the Cave Hill, Holders Green or Jackson bus
♿ Few
✋ Inexpensive

Above: *A sweet history of sugar making awaits at the Frank Hutson Sugar Museum*

The ABC Highway

Distance
5 miles (8km)

Time
Half a day

Start Point
Roundabout near University of
the West Indies
✚ 24A2

End Point
St. Lawrence Gap
✚ 24B1

Lunch
Excellent choice in St.
Lawrence Gap ($–$$$)

A drive along the modern Adams Barrow Cummins Highway (ABC) is a journey through Barbados's history. Many commuters head in and out of Bridgetown daily, so avoid morning and evening rush-hour traffic. At lunchtimes the traffic situation is better, and Sundays are ideal. The highway links the Grantley Adams International Airport with the west coast road up to Speightstown. It is named after three of the island's statesmen: Tom Adams (prime minister from 1976 to 1985); Errol Barrow (prime minister from 1966 to 1976 and 1986 to 1987); and Gordon Cummins (premier from 1958 to 1961).

Start at the roundabout near the University of the West Indies and take the ABC signposted route, heading eastwards.

You'll see traditional scenery of cane fields and chattel houses contrasting with the sleek buildings of telecommunications companies, car showrooms, banks and the island's television station. At the top of the St. Barnabas Highway is the *Freed Slave*, also known as Bussa. A heroic

"Bussa" the Freed Slave statue symbolizes the great emancipation

figure in the island's history, Bussa was blamed for leading the slave rebellion of 1816 in which many were killed, executed or deported. So long as you park safely and take care crossing the roundabout, you can reach the steps up to the statue base to take a photo.

Back at the roundabout, you can take a detour along Two Mile Hill towards Government House, once the home of John Pilgrim, a Quaker. The governor of Barbados lives there now. Get back on the ABC Highway and head south along St. Barnabas Highway to the roundabout just past the rent-a-car showroom. At the next roundabout go straight on to St. Lawrence Gap (➤ 56), a hive of souvenir shops, bars and cafés.

Park up and explore the Gap or go birdwatching in the Graeme Hall Bird Sanctuary (➤ 9).

What to See in the Central Heartland

DRAX HALL ✪

Regarded as one of the finest colonial mansions on the island and ranked as one of the oldest, Drax Hall was built by wealthy Sir James Drax and his brother William. It is thought to date from around 1650. Inside are magnificent oak carvings and a handsome staircase.

✚	25C2
✉	St. George
☎	433 2200
⏱	At time of writing the hall was closed to visitors and future openings unknown
♿	None

FLOWER FOREST AND ORCHID WORLD (➤ 18, TOP TEN)

FRANCIA PLANTATION HOUSE ✪✪

Built in the early 1900s. Francia Plantation House is one of the last of its kind to be built on the island. Because it is still occupied by descendants of its original owner, you get the homely atmosphere of a house that is actually lived in. Architecturally a mixture of European and Caribbean styles, the house has white walls and a cinnamon-colored roof. Tropical gardens and terraced lawns with fountains surround it. Inside, the house is paneled with Brazilian wood, and a Barbadian mahogany table and European chandelier can be seen in the dining room. Much of the furniture, fashioned by local craftsmen, and silver has been in the family for years. Of particular interest is the collection of antique maps and prints of the West Indies; the earliest is dated 1522. There are also 19th-century water-colours of Gun Hill Signal Station (➤ 71), which can be seen from the garden.

✚	24B2
✉	Near Gun Hill Signal Station, St. George
☎	429 0474
⏱	Mon–Fri 10–4
🚌	Several from Bridgetown (alight at Thorpes Cottage)
♿	Few
🍹	Moderate, complimentary drink included

Outside is a set of dripstones. Carved out of coral rock, they collected the rainwater which was then purified as it filtered though the coral. Early settlers to Barbados soon discovered this method for cleansing water, and even today the island's drinking water is purified naturally.

The splendid Francia Plantation House is engulfed by tropical plants

GUN HILL SIGNAL STATION ⭐⭐

Even if you've already visited Grenade Hall Signal Station
(➤ 38) and learnt about the signal stations' important role
in the early communications network of Barbados, Gun Hill
Signal Station is still worth a visit. It was built in 1818 and
was reputedly the cream of the string of stations established to warn of slave uprisings. Eventually they served as
lookouts for cargo ships. Restored by the Barbados
National Trust in 1982, Gun Hill, perched on a ridge
overlooking the St. George Valley and the south of the
island, features a gray flag tower. For travelers with time
it's a quiet place to while away a few hours or wait for the
best views, which occur around sunset. Look out for the
British Military Lion, a white figure carved from limestone
in the 19th century by the Adjutant-General of the Imperial
Forces, who was stationed on the island. A plaque below
the lion states his name and reads that the British lion shall
"…rule from the sea to the ends of the earth."

✚	24B2
✉	St. George
☎	429 1358
🕐	Mon–Sat 9–5
🍴	Café ($); opening hours restricted
🚌	From Bridgetown take the Sergeant Street bus
♿	Few
💵	Moderate

Below: *The limestone
figure of the British
Military Lion guards the
way to Gun Hill*

HARRISON'S CAVE (➤ 20, TOP TEN)

ST. GEORGE VALLEY ⭐

Francia Plantation House (➤ 69) overlooks the fertile St.
George Valley, an agricultural oasis coated with sugarcane
crops. St. George Parish Church stands proudly as one of
only four churches on the island to survive the hurricane of
1831. Built in 1784, the church boasts a splendid altar
painting called *Rise to Power*. It is the work of artist
Benjamin West, the first American president of the Royal
Academy. And remember the statue of Lord Nelson in
Bridgetown? Well, the sculptor, Richard Westmacott, also
created some sculptures here inside the church.

✚ 24B2

Opposite: *Gun Hill Signal
Station sits on a ridge
overlooking the fertile
St. George Valley*

71

✚ 25C3
✉ St. John
☎ 433 1524
◷ Daily
🚌 Bathsheba/East Coast bus

✚ 24B3
✉ St. Thomas
☎ 438 6671
◷ Daily 9–5 (except public hol)
🚌 From Bridgetown take the Sturges bus
♿ None
🖌 Moderate
❓ Wear good walking shoes and take drinking water

VILLA NOVA ✪

Yet another superb sugar boom mansion, Villa Nova, in St. John, was built in 1834 by Edmund Haynes at the center of his vast plantation. The late Sir Anthony Eden, a former British prime minister, bought the estate in 1965. A year later Queen Elizabeth II and Prince Philip sat down to lunch here during a public visit to the island. Now a luxury hotel—open to non-guests for drinks, meals and afternoon tea—the villa re-opened in April 2001 after a multi-million dollar refurbishment to restore its colonial heritage.

WELCHMAN HALL TROPICAL FOREST ✪✪

Formed by a series of caves that collapsed, the gully is a 0.62-mile (1-km) corridor of tropical jungle cutting through the coral foundations of the island. Cliffs rise up on either side, and banana, nutmeg and fig trees are among the 200 or so species of tropical plant that grow in the gully. It is said to take its name from a Welsh settler called Williams who once owned the land through which the ravine cuts. His descendants planted some of the specimen trees.

The National Trust, which takes care of the site, has added a few plants but it's pretty much left in a wild state. As you walk through, it is easy to imagine how Barbados must have looked before the first settlers arrived and carried out a program of ravaging deforestation. At one end a stalactite and stalagmite have met in the middle to form a 46-in (118-cm) diameter column that appears to be holding up the cliff. If you're present around dawn or dusk, you might spot Barbados green monkeys.

Amble through a corridor of tropical vegetation known as Welchman Hall Tropical Forest

Where To...

Above: *Champers Bar on
the south coast—a
favorite for wining and
dining*
Right: *Calypso and its
steel pan drums is
the music of
Barbados*

73

Bridgetown &
Around the Island

Price Categories

Prices are approximate, based on a three-course meal for one without drinks and service. Most restaurants include 15 percent VAT. A 10 percent service charge is extra.

$ = less than Bds$100
$$ = Bds$100–Bds$150
$$$ = over Bds$150

Bridgetown
Nelson Arms ($)

Here you'll find a mix of traditional English food—steaks and pies (steak and kidney for example) as well as Bajan fish dishes, also rice and burgers.

✉ Broad Street ☎ 431 0602 ⏰ Daily 8–6

Waterfront Café ($–$$)

Seafood specialties are served on tables spilling out onto the harborside. There's piano music on Tuesday in the afternoons and steel pan music or jazz from 7pm.

✉ Careenage ☎ 427 0093 ⏰ Mon–Sat 10am–midnight

East Coast
The Crane Lobster and Seafood Restaurant ($$–$$$)

(➤ 43) It's the view of a long stretch of beach on one side and a lavish pool on the other that makes dining at this hotel special, plus the fish and lobster. Among the notable dishes are seafood chowder and beef fillet cooked as you like it. Chubb, a specialty since 1887, is caught daily on the Crane Reef.

✉ The Crane ☎ 423 6220 ⏰ Daily 6.30pm–10pm

Edgewater Inn ($–$$)

Choose from a Bajan buffet at lunchtimes and Bajan specialties such as pepperpot stew and flying fish during the evening. Choose to dine on the terrace overlooking the surf-battered rocks, or inside in a wood-paneled restaurant with leaded windows.

✉ Bathsheba, St. Joseph ☎ 433 9900 ⏰ Lunch, dinner daily

South Coast
Bay Bistro ($$–$$$)

A casual bistro within the Yellow Bird Hotel overlooking St. Lawrence Bay. Serves international cuisine wih a Bajan flair, for breakfast, lunch and dinner. Live music and on Sundays, a roast beef and Yorkshire pudding lunch.

✉ St. Lawrence Gap, Christ Church ☎ 426 0059 ⏰ Lunch, dinner daily

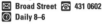Brown Sugar ($$–$$$)

A "planter's buffet luncheon" is served during the day and there is à la carte dining Creole-style every night, with a live jazz band playing on selected dates.

✉ Aquatic Gap, Needham's Point, St. Michael ☎ 426 7684 ⏰ Sun–Fri 12–2.30pm, daily from 6pm

Bubba's Sports Bar & Restaurant ($)

Air-conditioned eatery with satellite screens showing major sporting events, serving local and international cuisine.

✉ Rodeley, Christ Church ☎ 435 8731 ⏰ Lunch, dinner daily

Café Sol Mexican Grill and Margarita Bar ($–$$)

A crowded yet fashionable haunt, specializing in big plates of nachos, salads and the typical Mexican fare, plus tall cocktails and occasional offers such as two drinks for the price of one.

✉ St. Lawrence Gap, Christ Church ☎ 435 9531 ⏰ Lunch Tue–Sun, dinner daily

Champers ($–$$)

Set on the water's edge, this

popular wine bar and restaurant has a bistro downstairs and a pleasant dining room upstairs boasting fine views over the ocean.

✉ **Hastings, Christ Church**
☎ 435 6644 ⏲ **Lunch, dinner daily**

Croton Inn ($–$$)
Take your pick here from specials, curries, fish, and local specialty pudding and souse dish (pig, potatoes and pickle) on Saturday afternoons, and live jazz on occasions (➤ 82).

✉ **Maxwell Main Road, Christ Church** ☎ 428 7314
⏲ **Daily 6am-10.30pm**

▽▽▽Josef's ($$–$$$)
Extravagant seafood dishes and wines from around the world in his very classy signature restaurant by the beach.

✉ **St. Lawrence Gap, Christ Church** ☎ 435 8245 ⏲ **Daily 6.30pm–9.30/10pm**

Lucky HorseShoe ($–$$)
Open 24 hours for steaks, omelettes and waffles, a "trail blazing" BBQ buffet, US steaks, spare ribs, pasta, rice and potatoes. A favorite is the 280g (10oz) New Yorker grilled steak.

✉ **Worthing Main Road, Christ Church** ☎ 435 5825
⏲ **24 hours**

Oistins Fish Market ($)
(➤ 50) Amazing Fish Fry on Friday and Saturday evenings, when diners dance among the tables. At stalls and huts, freshly caught flying fish, dolphin, snapper, barbecued pig and chicken are cooked to take away or eat at handy benches and tables. No need to reserve a table, just turn up.

✉ **Oistins village, Christ Church** ⏲ **Mostly at night, some stalls are open throughout the day**

▽▽Opa's Greek Restaurant ($$–$$$)
Formerly the Shak Shak, famed for its setting by the ocean and its great views. It is now a Greek restaurant serving tasty Mediterranean dishes from the region.

✉ **Hastings, Christ Church** ☎ 435 1234 ⏲ **Daily from 6pm**

▽▽Pisces ($$–$$$)
Seafood terrace restaurant romantically set overlooking a sandy bay and cosily lit at night. Favorite dishes are conch fritters, fish chowder, snapper and blackened New York striploin.

✉ **St. Lawrence Gap, Christ Church** ☎ 435 6564 ⏲ **Daily from 6pm**

Ship Inn (Captain's Carvery $–$$)
The carvery offers a Bajan buffet at lunchtimes, and an English-style carvery (with big portions) in the evenings. Live bands play every night; Happy Hour 4–6pm and 10–11pm (➤ 83).

✉ **St. Lawrence Gap, Christ Church** ☎ 435 6961 ⏲ **Noon until at least 2am**

Steak House ($–$$)
Here US sizzling steaks are served on signature cast-iron "cows," and there's also a salad bar, pasta, seafood, chicken and lamb. On the same site, St. Lawrence Pizza Hut offers pizzas and hamburgers.

✉ **St. Lawrence Gap, Christ Church** ☎ 428 7152
⏲ **Daily 9am–11pm**

Buffets
Bajan buffets ($–$$) are available in many bars and restaurants. Help yourself to fried plantains, macaroni cheese pie, pumpkin, pork or chicken, flying fish, beetroot, coleslaw, *cou-cou* (➤ 52) – and go back for more if you're still not satisfied.

Fast Food

Chefette Restaurants are Barbados's answer to MacDonalds. They sell fast-fried burgers, spare ribs, steak, chicken nuggets and fries cheaply and quickly. Salads, baked potatoes, rice and macaroni pies are extras. Thirteen Chefettes are dotted around the island, some of which have drive-throughs and barbecue barns. A few also have children's playgrounds.

🍷Sweet Potatoes ($–$$)

Friendly, clean and well-priced restaurant with good food and cocktails. Happy hour 10–11pm.
📧 St. Laurence Gap, Christ Church ☎ 435 9638 ⏰ Daily

🍷🍷Wytukai ($$)

Exotic Polynesian atmosphere as you dine in an indigenous-style hut. Polynesian food and music.
📧 Accra Beach Hotel, Christ Church ☎ 435 8920 ⏰ Tue–Sat 6.30pm–11.30

Zafran ($$$)

Unique to Barbados, this authentic Indian restaurant is housed in an elegant mansion house set in extensive gardens with mango and coconut trees. Excellent Indian, Persian and Thai dishes are prepared by award-winning chefs and served in luxury surroundings, but not necessarily at luxury prices.
📧 El Sueno, Worthing Main Road, Worthing ☎ 435 8995 ⏰ Daily

West Coast

L'Acajou ($$$)

Sandy Lane's main restaurant re-designed by internationally acclaimed David Collins is now well established. Formal dining on the terrace with sea views. European fare with hints of Asia.
📧 Sandy Lane, St. James ☎ 444 2030 ⏰ Daily 6.30–10pm

Calabaza ($$$)

Moroccan-style architecture, overlooking the ocean creating a very romantic atmosphere. Mix of Eastern and Western cooking.
📧 Prospect St. James ☎ 424 4557 ⏰ Dinner daily

Carambola ($–$$)

An outstanding setting on a cliff above the sea and Caribbean dishes influenced by France and Asia make this a favorite with Bajans.
📧 Derrick's, St. James ☎ 432 0832 ⏰ Mon–Sat 6.30pm–9.30pm

🍷🍷🍷The Cliff ($$$)

Regarded as the finest, most expensive and most exclusive restaurant on the island, The Cliff has a neo-classical, tiered dining terrace overlooking the sea. Each dish is a masterpiece. Booked up for months in advance.
📧 Derrick's, St. James ☎ 432 1922 ⏰ Dinner Mon–Sat 6.30–9.30

Cobbler's Cove (Terrace Restaurant $$$)

A well-recommended Relais et Chateaux restaurant within Cobbler's Cove Hotel. Continental food with a Caribbean accent is prepared by French-trained chefs and served on a lamplit terrace by the sea. Great cocktails and a renowned wine list are highlights. Reservations essential.
📧 Cobbler's Cove, St. Peter ☎ 422 2291 ⏰ Daily 12.30–2.30, 6.30–9 (Tue BBQ/buffet night). Regular live music

🍷🍷🍷Daphne's ($$)

Grilled specials and seafoods feature at this well decorated restaurant, sister to Daphne's in London. Famous cocktails and an extensive wine list.

☒ **Payre's Bay** ☎ **432 2731**
◉ **Daily**

The Fish Pot ($$$)
A regular haunt for A-list celebrities who dine at this water's edge resaurant in part of a converted fort on the beach.
☒ **Little Good Harbour, Sherman's** ☎ **439 2604/3000**
◉ **Daily 12–3, 6.30–9.15**

▽▽▽Lone Star ($$–$$$)
Stylish beach restaurant offering Mediterranean, modern European and traditional Caribbean dishes, served alfresco.
☒ **Mount Standfast, St. James** ☎ **419 0599** ◉ **Daily 11.30–3.30, 6–10**

Mango's By the Sea ($$)
A Canadian-owned place overlooking the ocean and known for its lobster bisque and grilled lobster. Also serves New York striploin steak and barbecued back ribs followed by homemade desserts and excellent espresso.
☒ **By the sea, Speightstown, St. Peter** ☎ **422 0704**
◉ **Daily from 6pm**

Olives Bar and Bistro ($$–$$$)
Cozy garden patio bistro with tables laid out under fairy lights. It is famous for its yellow fin tuna steaks with ratatouille or jerked pork and scorched onions in generous portions.
☒ **2nd Street, Holetown, St. James** ☎ **432 2112**
◉ **Nightly 6.30–9.30**

Palm Terrace ($$$)
(► 60) Grand, formal restaurant within the Fairmont Royal Pavilion

serving international food on fine china at candlelit tables. White cotton-covered chairs, occasional live music playing in the background and the sound of the lapping waves add to the atmosphere.
☒ **Fairmont Royal Pavilion Hotel, St. James** ☎ **422 5555**
◉ **Mon–Sat 7am–9.45pm. Afternoon tea ($) for non-guests served 3.30–5**

Patisserie Flindt ($)
Check out the succulent pastries, puddings, breads and homemade chocolates while sipping cappuccino. Alternatively, try the excellent freshly made sandwiches and sausage rolls, or buy a tub of Häagen-Dazs ice cream.
☒ **1st Street, Holetown, St. James** ☎ **432 2626** ◉ **Mon–Fri 7am–5pm, Sat 7am–2pm, Sun (in season) 7am–midnight**

Sugar Sugar Beach Bar ($$–$$$)
A great setting above the coral sands of one of the most famous beaches on Barbados. Choose from light lunches to romantic candlelit dinners.
☒ **Mullins Bay, St. Peter** ☎ **419 4511** ◉ **Daily 11–4, 6–10**

▽▽▽The Tides ($$$)
Set on the water's edge overlooking the sea with an excellent menu of chowders, salads, pasta, seafood and the fresh catch of the day. Try the bistro-style restaurant inside for casual dining or the terrace outside for a more romantic setting in lush gardens.
☒ **Holetown, St. James** ☎ **432 8356** ◉ **Lunch Mon–Fri, dinner Mon–Sat**

Dress Code
Elegant, casual dress is encouraged at nearly all restaurants. More formal attire is required for the upmarket restaurants, so check before you dine. Anywhere other than the beach, bikinis, shorts and undershirts (vests) are not accepted.

Around the Island

Price Categories

Prices are for a double room, excluding breakfast, in the high season (December 16–April 15). Expect to pay a third less, sometimes half price, for the rest of the year. Prices exclude 7½ percent VAT and 10–15 percent service charge. These prices may be lower if you book as part of a package holiday.

$ = under US$200
$$ = US$200–400
$$$ = over US$400

Bridgetown Hotels

Hotels are found on the west, south and east coasts. Bridgetown itself has no tourist hotels though there are plenty of choices of accommodations minutes away, on the coastal roads that branch out from the capital.

Hotel Services

Standard services offered by hotels are generally European Plan (EP) room only or Modified American Plan (MAP), including breakfast and dinner.

East Coast

▼▼▼The Crane ($$$)

(► 43) This 18th-century hotel perched on a cliff overlooks a pink bay, one of the island's most famous beaches.

✉ St. Philip ☎ 423 6220/fax 423 5343

Edgewater Inn ($)

Set on a ledge overlooking the Atlantic crashing on to rock formations below, the Edgewater is only a few steps from Bathsheba beach. Voted Best Small Hotel by readers of *Caribbean Life* magazine. Activities include nature walks and yoga.

✉ Bathsheba beach ☎ 433 9900/fax 433 9902

Sam Lord's Castle and Resort ($$)

(► 44) Built for the notorious Sam Lord, now an all-inclusive resort where most rooms have king-size beds and a balcony or a patio overlooking the Atlantic. Sam Lord's own bedroom is available.

✉ St. Philip ☎ 423 7350/fax 423 5981

South Coast

▼▼▼Accra Beach Hotel & Resort ($–$$)

An elegant hotel set on a spectacular beach of soft white sands—cocktail parties, barbecues and floor shows. New wing of suites and pool suites, now open.

✉ Christ Church ☎ 435 8920/fax 435 6794

▼▼▼Bougainvillea Beach Resort ($$–$$$)

Overlooking the Caribbean Sea on a luxury resort with suites and kitchen facilities.

Restaurants, kids' club, pool, watersports and tennis.

✉ Christ Church ☎ 418 0990/fax 1428 2524

Rockley Plumtree Club ($)

A resort condominium and apartments to rent nestled in lush, tropical gardens and close to restaurants. Pool.

✉ Christ Church ☎ 435 7606/fax 435 8282

Silver Rock Hotel ($$)

The only all-inclusive resort within the Gems of Barbados group, this is a stylish resort for the fashionable young and sporty. From the Jibboom open-air restaurant you're given a grandstand view of a slice of the Atlantic renowned for its windsurfing. You'll see many professional windsurfers out on the breakers and can arrange your own lessons from the resident windsurfing champion.

✉ Silver Sands beach, Christ Church ☎ 428 2866/fax 428 3687

Turtle Beach ($$)

All-inclusive family resort with a brilliant Tommy Turtle kids club for 3–12 year olds and plenty to do for couples as well. It has elegant restaurants and suites, plus live floor shows.

✉ St. Lawrence Gap ☎ 428 7131/fax 428 6089

West Coast

▼▼ZAlmond Beach Villas ($$–$$$)

An all-inclusive resort comprising seven villages within an historic sugar plantation, originally built in 1865, close by the sea. Ideal for families, with a spa, keep-fit classes, tennis and golf lessons, and masses of children's facilities.

✉ **St. Peter** ☎ **422 4900/fax 422 0617**

⬤⬤⬤**Cobbler's Cove ($$$)**
Pink turrets rising from manicured, tropical green foliage distinguish this Relais et Chateaux property perched above coral sands. Cottages and suites, furnished with cottons and rattan furniture, open on to gardens or the sea. The ultimate, though, is a seafront suite with rooftop plunge pool. There is a small fitness center and boutique.

✉ **St. Peter** ☎ **422 2291/fax 422 1460**

⬤⬤⬤**Colony Club ($$$)**
A former gentleman's club, the Colony is now a sophisticated hotel with an old Englishness and charm catering to couples and families. The extensive tropical gardens include four freshwater pools.

✉ **Porters, St. James** ☎ **422 2335/fax 422 0667**

⬤⬤⬤**Fairmont Glitter Bay ($$$)**
(➤ 60). Formerly the home of shipping magnate Sir Edward Cunard (the main beach house dates from the 1630s), Fairmont Glitter Bay shares a 30-acre (12-ha) beachfront estate with the Royal Pavilion (➤ below). Inclusive activities include tennis, watersports and signing privileges at the Royal Westmoreland Golf Course.

✉ **Porters, St. James** ☎ **422 555/fax 422 1367**

⬤⬤ ⬤⬤**Fairmont Royal Pavilion Hotel ($$$)**
(➤ 60). Although a

beachfront resort, this rose-pink, graceful top-price establishment is very private. It is shrouded in tropical gardens so diverse that it takes a botanical tour (held weekly) to explain the species. Enjoy the afternoon tea of cakes and cucumber sandwiches, served in a traditional, 30s English style.

✉ **Porters, St. James** ☎ **422 5555/422 0118**

⬤⬤⬤**The House at Tamarind Cove ($$$)**
A very exclusive sanctuary for luxury and privacy. The hotel has just 32 rooms, and ambassadors, who are similar to butlers, on hand to provide the best service.

✉ **Paynes Bay, St. James**
☎ **432 5525/fax 432 5255**

⬤⬤⬤**The Sandpiper ($$$)**
Just 20 minutes from Bridgetown, this charming beachfront hotel, set amid landscaped grounds, offers individual suites for families and couples. Facilities include a top-class restaurant, pool, tennis and watersports. Member of the Small Luxury Hotels of the World.

✉ **Holetown, St. James**
☎ **422 2251/fax 422 1776**

⬤⬤ ⬤⬤**Sandy Lane Hotel Golf Club ($$$)**
Unashamed luxury, this famous hotel has accommodated royalty and movie stars in its luxurious rooms and suites since 1961. The Palladian-style cream coral stone buildings are situated in a beautiful 800-acre (324-ha) beachfront estate.

✉ **St. James** ☎ **444 2000/fax 444 2222**

Hotel Chains
The Elegant Hotels group dominates a large proportion of the luxury hotels market on Barbados and is therefore the largest. It invested US$5million in The House at Tamarind Cove on the west coast. The other properties are Colony Club, Crystal Cove and Turtle Beach. Gems of Barbados is another hotel chain with five properties on the south coast, including the Silver Rock Hotel on the famous windsurfing paradise of Silver Sands.

Day Passes
At some all-inclusive resorts non-residents can buy a day pass, but check the watersports are not fully booked. A few have a nursery or kids' club where you can leave the children while you enjoy the watersports and bars.

Arts, Handicrafts & Department Stores

Opening Times
Despite the number of tourists you'll find that many shops close on Sundays. As a general rule, most shops and stores in major areas are open Mon–Fri 9–5 and until 1pm on Saturdays. Larger stores in Bridgetown are open until 6pm daily and 4pm Saturday.

Endangered Species
Beware the souvenirs made from protected species, such as turtle shell souvenirs, black coral pieces and jewelry. Not only does buying them encourage destruction of the natural environment, but you risk being fined. Products containing the feathers of parrots and other birds may also be illegal. Think twice about buying a queen conch shell, which is important to Caribbean seagrass ecosystems.

Art & Handicrafts

Chalky Mount Village
(► 17, Top Ten)

Chattel House Shopping Village
Colorful chattel-style houses crammed with souvenirs and beachwear bearing slogans such as "Jammin' in de Street."
🖂 **St. Lawrence Gap, Christ Church (also at Holetown)**
☎ **428 2472** 🕐 **Mon–Sat 9–6**

Earthworks and the Potters House
(► 58) See pottery, from bowls to ornaments, being made and hand-decorated. Also clay, metalwork, glass and fabric designs.
🖂 **Edgehill, St. Thomas**
☎ **425 0223** 🕐 **Mon–Fri 9–5, Sat 9–1**

Kirby Gallery
A good place to pick up original art and limited-edition prints by local and international artists.
🖂 **The Courtyard, Hastings, Christ Church** ☎ **430 3032**
🕐 **Mon–Fri 9–1, 2–5**

Mango's Fine Art Gallery
Works by local artist Michael Adams, who grew up in Africa and graduated from the Royal College of Art, London.
🖂 **Queen Street, Speightstown**
☎ **422 0704** 🕐 **Daily 6pm–11.30pm**

Medford Craft Village
Woodcarvers create items from the mahogany trees and roots that surround them. Showroom with a host of Barbadian crafts.
🖂 **Barbarees Hill, St. Michael**
☎ **427 3179** 🕐 **Daily 9–5 (Sat until 2)**

Pelican Craft Village
Eight attractive shops display pottery, woodwork, glassware and paintings.
🖂 **Princess Alice Highway, Bridgetown** ☎ **427 5350**
🕐 **Mon–Fri 9–5, Sat 9–2pm.**
Extended hours in peak season

Shell Gallery
An outstanding collection of shells from around the world.
🖂 **Gills, St. Peter** ☎ **422 2593**
🕐 **Mon–Fri 9–5, Sat 9–2**

Stony Hill Studios
Works by Lilian Sten-Nicholson, known for her paintings of steel band music.
🖂 **Stony Hill Studio, St. Philip**
☎ **423 6237** 🕐 **Open by appointment**

Stores & Malls

Cave Shepherd
International merchandise at tax-free prices.
🖂 **Broad Street, Bridgetown and Grantley Adams Airport**
🕐 **Mon–Sat**

Cave Shepherd Sunset Crest Mall
Souvenirs, clothing, gifts, crafts and oddments.
🖂 **Sunset Crest Plaza No. 2, Holetown** 🕐 **Mon–Sat**

DaCostas Mall
Pink-and-white colonial building with more than 20 shops, including a tax-free camera shop and food court.
🖂 **Broad Street, Bridgetown**
🕐 **Mon–Sat 9–5**

Sheraton Centre
Some 75 shops for clothing, gifts and electrical goods.
🖂 **Life of Barbados Roundabout, near St. Lawrence, Christ Church** 🕐 **Mon–Sat 9–9**

Food, Jewellery, Markets & Souvenirs

Food & Supermarkets

Big B
Fresh meat, fruit, vegetables, a deli, a French bakery, a pharmacy and a bank, all in one place.
✉ **Peronne Plaza, Worthing**
☎ **435 7927** 🕐 **Mon–Thu 8–8, Fri, Sat 8–9**

Gourmet Shop at Chattel House Village
Everything from Bajan hot sauce, nutmeg and vanilla beans to hand-rolled Cuban cigars and aged Bourbons.
✉ **Chattel Village, Holetown**
☎ **432 7711** 🕐 **Mon–Sat 9–5.30**

Liquor
Rum, beer and other island drinks can be bought from:
Banks (Breweries) ➤ **48; Rum Distilleries** ➤ **49 and 50; Arrivals Duty Free Shop at Grantley Adams Airport**

Jewelry

Colombian Emeralds International
Duty-free jewels from around the Caribbean, and emeralds from Colombia.
✉ **Broad Street, Bridgetown; Grantley Adams Airport; Cruise Terminal; Almond Beach Village**
☎ **1 800 6NO DUTY** 🕐 **Varies**

Diamonds International Barbados
Have a diamond mounted and set before you leave .
✉ **Broad Street, Cave Shepherd in Bridgetown; Fairmont Glitter Bay Hotel in St. James; Grantley Adams Airport**
☎ **430 2400** 🕐 **Mon–Sat**

Galleria
Broad range of beautiful emerald, diamond and gemstone jewelry; designer Italian gold and exquisite watches.
✉ **Sandy Lane Golf & Country Club, St. James** ☎ **419 4505**
🕐 **Various**

Royal Shop
Jewelry, plus hand-sculpted figurines from Tuscany in Italy.
✉ **Broad Street, Bridgetown**
☎ **429 7072** 🕐 **Mon–Fri 9–4.30, Sat 9–2.30**

Markets
Barbados isn't noted for its markets, but the Saturday morning Cheapside Fruit Market (Lower Broad Street, Bridgetown) offers fruit, handicrafts, jewelry and Rastafarian oddments. In Speightstown fruit and veg stalls line the main street. Other markets include Oistins Fish Market (➤ 51), Oistins, Christ Church—daily and the Rastafarian Street Market, Temple Yard, Bridgetown—daily.

Souvenirs

Best of Barbados Gift Shops
Gift shops throughout Barbados that specialize in prints and gifts made or designed on the island, carefully selected for their craftsmanship and value for money.

Flamboya
Hand-painted, hand-dyed and appliquéd clothing, plus batiks.
✉ **DaCosta's Mall, Broad Street, Bridgetown and Hastings Plaza, Christ Church** ☎ **431 0022** 🕐 **Mon–Fri 8.30–5, Sat 8.30–3**

Duty Free
Duty-free shopping is available in various well-respected shops, on production of your passport and/or travel documents. Goods that cannot be bought duty-free over the counter—and therefore delivered to the airport for pick-up before boarding—are spirits, wines, tobacco, cigarettes, cigars, video sets, video games, videotapes, car stereos, televisions and home computers.

Bars, Clubs & Shows

Nightspots

St. Lawrence Gap (➤ 56), Christ Church, is recognized as the throbbing heart of Barbados, packed with clubs, bars and restaurants open until late. Happy Hours, with two drinks for the price of one, are usually hosted early evening. It is fashionable not to arrive at a nightclub before 10pm and it's even better if you get there around midnight. Local live bands are highly talented.

Traditional Sounds

The most popular bands in the early history of post-emancipation were the Bumbalum or Took (tuk) bands who traveled from village to village playing a type of music that mimicked the English military band sound, yet had roots in African beats.

Bars & Clubs

39 Steps Wine Bar

Relaxing wine bar with a sophisticated atmosphere and live jazz every other Saturday night.

✉ **Chattel Plaza, Hastings, Christ Church** ☎ **427 0715** 🕐 **Mon–Fri noon–midnight, Sat 6pm–midnight**

After Dark

Popular nightclub with indoor and outdoor dance floors. DJ, Caribbean rhythms. Quieter jazz club. Regular live bands.

✉ **Christ Church** ☎ **435 6457** 🕐 **Fri, Sat night**

Bert's Bar

Catch up with the sports and world news live on satellite television. Popular slot machines and a famous daiquiri drink.

✉ **Rockley, Christ Church** ☎ **435 7924** 🕐 **Daily until 1am, Happy Hour Mon–Fri 4.30–6pm**

Boatyard

Live bands, DJs and special events, with "free drinks" deals.

✉ **St. Michael** ☎ **436 2622** 🕐 **9am–late**

Bubba's Sports Bar

Live sports, from soccer to baseball, via two satellite dishes on large TV screens.

✉ **Rockley, Christ Church** ☎ **435 6217** 🕐 **24 hours**

Casbah

Moroccan-style nightclub with DJ music and regular live music. Dress code. Valet parking.

✉ **Baku beach, Holetown** ☎ **432 2258** 🕐 **Thu–Sat 10pm–4am**

Casuarina Beach Club

Regular live music by local bands, a steel orchestra and special West Indian floor shows.

✉ **St. Lawrence Gap** ☎ **428 3600** 🕐 **24 hours**

Club Skyy

New nightclub with the latest sounds and dance trends.

✉ **Spring Garden, St. Michael** ☎ **421 7599** 🕐 **Thu–Sat from 10pm**

Coach House

Live sports from around the world via satellite.

✉ **Paynes Bay, St. James** ☎ **432 1163** 🕐 **24 hours; Happy Hour 5–7pm**

Croton Inn

Live jazz by a range of artists is played on the first Sunday of the month (➤ 75).

✉ **Maxwell Main Road, Christ Church** ☎ **428 7314** 🕐 **24 hours**

Harbour Lights

Massively popular beach-front club. Monday is Beach Party with BBQ, exotic drinks, limbo and fire-eating. Wednesdays and Fridays are pay once, drinks free. Dance under the stars or indoors. The only nightspot where beachwear is acceptable, in fact, here it's a must!

✉ **Bay Street, St. Michael** ☎ **436 7225** 🕐 **Mon, Wed, Fri, from 9.30pm–very late**

McBridges Pub and Cookhouse

Live music from simple acoustic guitars and singers to bands, karaoke and reggae.

✉ **St. Lawrence Gap** ☎ **435 6352** 🕐 **Daily, music 10pm–late**

Le Mirage

Offers reggae music on the weekends with themed nights during the week. Gets very lively after midnight.

✉ **Cavans Lane, Bridge House** ☎ **428 8115** ⏰ **9pm–late**

Reggae Lounge

Reggae, calypso and other Caribbean hits played by the island's DJs to a packed dance floor. Regular live bands.

✉ **St. Lawrence Gap** ☎ **435 6462** ⏰ **Nightly**

Ship Inn

Traditional English-style pub with satellite sports from around the world and live music nightly, covering all bases from calypso to rock and soul. Karaoke is also a favorite.

✉ **St. Lawrence Gap** ☎ **435 6961** ⏰ **Daily until late; Happy Hour 4–6pm, 10–11pm**

Waterfront Café

Lunchtime piano on Tuesdays, and either CD background jazz, live jazz, or steel pan music and singing on selected evenings.

✉ **The Careenage, Bridgetown** ☎ **427 0093** ⏰ **24 hours**

Whistling Frog

Solid street pub with occasional live music and DJ.

✉ **St. Lawrence Gap** ☎ **420 5021** ⏰ **24 hours**

Weisers on the Bay Beach Bar and Restaurant

Lots of ice-cold Banks bottled beer accompanied by good music. The meals are good too (➤ 77).

✉ **Brandons, Spring Garden Highway West Coast** ☎ **425 6450** ⏰ **Day and night**

Shows

Bajan Roots & Rhythms

A Caribbean show and dinner party, buffet and unlimited drinks.

✉ **Plantation Theatre, St. Lawrence** ☎ **428 5048** ⏰ **Various, phone to book**

The Crane

(➤ 43) Amazing gospel singing and brunch.

✉ **St. Philip** ☎ **423 6220** ⏰ **Sun 9.30–noon**

Fisherman's Pub and Beach Bar

The Sunset steel orchestra and floor show is on regularly, plus Bajan buffet every Wednesday evening.

✉ **Speightstown, St Peter** ☎ **422 2703** ⏰ **Open for drinks nightly**

Harbour Master Cruises

Evening dinner cruise featuring floor show of belly dancing, limbo and calypso.

✉ **From Shallow Draught, Bridgetown** ☎ **430 0900** ⏰ **Various nights; reservations essential**

Jolly Roger Party Cruise

Fun sail on the wooden schooner; rope swing and snorkel. Rum included.

✉ **From Shallow Draught, Bridgetown** ☎ **430 0900** ⏰ **Various, phone to book Thu and Sat**

Tropical Spectacular Show

Dinner show with carnival costumes, dance, music, fire-eating, limbo and a Bajan buffet. Reservations essential. Bajan Roots and Rhythms Show.

✉ **St. Lawrence main road** ☎ **428 5048** ⏰ **Wed, Fri from 6.30pm**

Karaoke

One of the best nights out on Barbados is to visit a local karaoke, Caribbean and Reggae style, where everyone wants to be Bob Marley.

Theater

Performances are held throughout the year at the following venues.

Frank Collymore Hall
Sir Garfield Sobers Gymnasium
Daphne Joseph Hacket Theatre
Plantation Theatre

Check with the daily newspapers for what's on, or ☎ 427 2623 (Tourist Information)

Activities, Sports & Children's Attractions

Setting Sail
Stay close to the island or head out to the other Caribbean islands of Antigua, Martinique, Grenada, the Grenadines, St. Vincent, Tobago and Trinidad. If money is no object, then the ocean's the limit. Either charter your own yacht and captain and go deep-sea fishing, or rent a fully trained crew, a good chef, and a luxurious catamaran for your private party, romantic dinner or snorkelling.

Value for Money
The smaller Christ Church hotels of Butterfly Beach, Dover Beach, Peach and Quiet, Windsurf Beach and Woodville Beach have joined forces to develop "Added Value Packages," which include ecotourism walks, sports and watersports packages and golfing breaks.

Athletics
The National Stadium, just outside Bridgetown, can hold 5,000 fans for soccer, cycling and other events.
☎ 426 0627

Cricket
Regional season January to March. The international season April to May.
✉ Kensington Oval, Bridgetown ☎ 436 1397

Cruises

Foster & Ince
Cruise company to various islands and beyond.
☎ 431 8914

MV Harbour Master
A four-deck high steamboat-style cruiser for both day and night cruises.
☎ 430 0990

Ocean Adventures Silver Moon Sailing Cruises
Aboard the luxury catamaran Silver Moon (maximum of 12) for a shared cruise.
☎ 233 7626/436 2088

Deep-sea Fishing
Boats for half or full day charters. Popular catches are sailfish, tuna, blue marlin and barracuda.

Fishing Charters Barbados Inc
☎ 429 2326

Golf

Barbados Golf Club
In the south of Durrants close to the airport. A new course, coaching schools and club house. Pay-as-you-play.
✉ Durrants, Christ Church
☎ 428 8463

Rockley Golf Course
A pleasant 9-hole course close to the south coast.
✉ Rockley, Christ Church
☎ 435 7873

Royal Westmoreland
The exclusive 18-hole Robert Trent-Jones II championship course is a private course but does have limited openings on pay-as-you-play.
✉ St. James ☎ 422 4653

Sandy Lane Country Club Course
Open to all golfers on a pay-as-you-play basis. Stunning views of the west coast.
✉ St. James ☎ 444 2000

Helicopter Tours

Bridgetown Heliport
Air-conditioned jet helicopters whisk you along the Caribbean coastline and over to the east, for either 20 or 30 minutes. Reserve in advance.
✉ Bridgetown ☎ 431 0069

Hiking

National Trust
Offers regular guided walks and Sunday strolls.
☎ 425 2020/426 2421

Horse-racing

Barbados Turf Club
Race meetings are held at the Garrison Savannah on Saturday throughout the year including premier thorough-bred races. Spectator packages include lunch and drinks in the air-conditioned restaurant with views of the racetrack, grandstand seats, transfers from hotel and betting vouchers.
☎ 426 3980

Horse Riding
There are several good riding stables on the island.

Caribbean International Riding
☎ 422 7433

Highland Adventure Centre
Horse riding, mountain bikes, hiking. Free hotel pick-up.
☎ 438 8069

Safari Tours
4WD Journey on a tour of the island, including Mount Hillaby and sugar estates.

Island Safari
☎ 429 5337

Scuba Diving
PADI certified courses and dives to reefs and wrecks along the west and south coasts. Equipment to rent.

Hightide
☎ 432 0931

Ocean Adventures
Kayaking and snorkelling. Also "Snuba" (▶ 59).
☎ 233 7626/436 2088

Surfing & Windsurfing

Club Mistral
Ttwo centers; intermediate level and jump novices.
✉ Oistins ☎ 248 7277
🕐 Nov–Jun, 9–5

Silver Rock
Windsurfing, surfing, kiteboarding. Wave novices and experts.
✉ Silver Sands ☎ 428 2366

Surfing Barbados School
For adults and children.
✉ Long Beach, Christ Church
☎ 228 5117

Children's Attractions & Activities

Atlantis Submarine
(▶ 57) A real submarine taking day and night dives to the bottom of the sea, with views of coral gardens, wrecks and tropical fish.
✉ Shallow Draught, Bridgetown ☎ 436 8929

Barbados Golf Club
Chipping green and practise net for the not-so-serious golfer, whatever age.
✉ Balls, Christ Church
☎ 428 8463

Barbados Wildlife Reserve
(▶ 14) Watch tortoises roam freely around the reserve and rabbits hop around the iguanas in the pen. Barbados green monkeys swing through the trees around 2–3pm.
✉ Farley Hill, St. Peter
☎ 422 8826 🕐 Daily 10–5 (3.45 last admission)

Kayak & Turtle Adventure
After a scenic powerboat, ride enjoy a kayak tour along the west coast and learn about Barbados. At Turtle Bay learn about the turtles and their living habits.
☎ 233 7626

Ocean Park
This new aquarium attraction, geared toward families, takes an educational slant. See fish and marine life from the Caribbean, a living reef, ray pool and touch pool and feeding demonstrations. Restaurant and bar.
✉ Balls, Christ Church
☎ 420 7405 🕐 Daily from 9am

Children's Safety
• At some all-inclusive resorts, parents can buy a day pass and leave their children in a supervised nursery or club that organizes painting and playing activities.
• When choosing a place to swim, always check it is safe. The south coast especially has strong Atlantic currents. The east coast is not suitable for swimming at all.
• Body boards are cheap to hire and great fun, as is snorkeling gear.
• Make sure children are well covered in high-factor suncream, and toddlers especially should wear a sunhat.

What's On When

Calypso

Calypso is the music of Barbados, played by steel pan bands. Drums were banned by the Church and the plantation owners, so the sugarcane slaves communicated with other workers on oil drums. Buy a CD to keep Barbados alive in your memory.

January

Barbados Jazz Festival (mid-month)—a weekend of sounds from local and visiting Caribbean jazz performers.
Windsurfing Championship held on Silver Sands. The horse-racing season at the Garrison Savannah gets underway.

February

The Holetown Festival (second week) has been going for over 20 years and is now one of the island's biggest events. It celebrates the arrival of English settlers and African slaves to the island in 1627. Street fairs and music, plus a beauty show with entrants competing for the Miss Holetown title.

March/April

The Holders Opera Season (lasts two weeks) of opera, music and theater draws world-wide audiences.
For atmosphere, the Oistins Fish Festival (Easter) is a must. The event features fishing, racing and a fish-boning competition. Stalls sell local arts and crafts and there's singing, dancing, the flavorsome Fish Fry and plenty of rum.
Barbados Sandy Lane Gold Cup, main event of the horse-racing season, held at the Garrison Savannah.
The end of April sees the Congaline Carnival, centered on "De Congaline Village" in a playing field near St. Lawrence Gap. The idea is to create the Caribbean's longest Conga line and there's a street party atmosphere throughout the nine-day festival.

May

Attracting singers and musicians from the United States and the rest of the Caribbean, Gospelfest is held on Whitsun weekend.
The Mount Gay Barbados Regatta, with around 30 of the top Caribbean yachts, takes place.

June/July

Crop Over Festival (end June/early July to August) is the highlight of the Barbados calendar. Originating on the sugar plantations when workers celebrated the end of the harvest, it was revived in 1974. The festival starts with a ceremonial delivery of the last canes of the harvest and bursts into a flurry of fairs, concerts and parades. During the Calypso Competition the latest calypso king or queen is crowned. ☎ 424 0909 for list of cultural events.

August

Emancipation Day (1st) when slavery was abolished on the island.
Grand Kadooment Day on the first Monday, when the Crop Over Festival bursts into the biggest party of the year with a huge carnival.

November

To coincide with the independence celebrations (November 30 is Independence Day and a national holiday), the National Independence Festival of Creative Arts runs throughout the month, with singing, dancing, acting and writing competitions. The festival culminates with a gala presentation.

Practical Matters

Above: *Bright and breezy,
the Mini Moke is a popular
choice of rental car*
Right: *Fresh coconuts for
drinking are sold by the roadside*

GMT 12 noon	Barbados 8am	Germany 1pm	USA (NY) 7am	Netherlands 1pm	Spain 1pm

BEFORE YOU GO

WHAT YOU NEED

	UK	Germany	USA	Netherlands	Spain
Passport valid for 6 months beyond date of departure/national ID card	●	●	●	●	●
Visa (regulations can change—check before booking your trip)	▲	▲	▲	▲	▲
Onward or return ticket	●	●	●	●	●
Health inoculations (polio, tetanus, typhoid, hepatitis A)	○	○	○	○	○
Health documentation (► 91, Health)	○	○	○	○	○
Travel insurance	○	○	○	○	○
Driving license (current or international)	●	●	●	●	●
Car insurance certificate (if own car)	○	○	○	○	○
Car registration document (if own car)	▲	▲	▲	▲	▲

- ● Required
- ○ Suggested
- ▲ Not required

Some countries require a passport to remain valid for a minimum period (usually at least six months) beyond the date of entry—contact their consulate or embassy or your travel agent for details.

WHEN TO GO

Barbados

■ High season

☐ Low season (June to November is the official hurricane season)

27°C	27°C	17°C	27°C	27°C	27°C	31°C	31°C	27°C	27°C	27°C	27°C
JAN	FEB	MAR	APR	MAY	JUN	JUL	AUG	SEP	OCT	NOV	DEC

☀ Sun   ⛅ Sun/showers   🌧 Wet

TOURIST OFFICES

In the UK
Barbados Tourism
Authority
263 Tottenham Court Road
London
W1P 0LA
☎ 020 7636 9448
Fax 020 7637 1496

In the USA
Barbados Tourism
Authority
800 Second Avenue
2nd Floor
New York
NY 10017
☎ 212 986 6516

Toll Free 1 800 221 9831

CONSULATES

UK
436 6694

Germany
427 1876

Netherlands
418 8074

USA
436 4950

WHEN YOU ARE THERE

ARRIVING

Visitors arrive at Grantley Adams International Airport in the south. It is the island's only airport. Cruise passengers dock at the Deep Water harbor in Bridgetown, at the swish Cruise Passenger Terminal with duty free shopping, banking and other facilities.

Grantley Adams International Airport
9 miles (15km) to city center

CUSTOMS

YES

1 liter of spirits
200 cigarettes **or**
250 grammes of tobacco **or**
50 cigars

Gifts are subject to tax duty.

MONEY

Barbados's currency is the Barbados dollar (Bds$), divided into 100 cents. Both US and Barbados dollars are accepted, and major credit cards can be used at most hotels, restaurants and stores. International banks include Barclays Bank plc and Canadian Imperial Bank of Commerce. At Grantley Adams International Airport, the Barbados Bank is open daily from 8am until the last flight departs.

NO

Drugs, firearms, ammunition, offensive weapons, obscene material, unlicensed animals.

OPENING HOURS

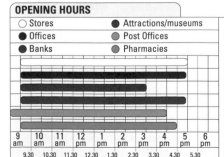

○ Stores	● Attractions/museums
● Offices	● Post Offices
● Banks	● Pharmacies

| 9 am | 10 am | 11 am | 12 pm | 1 pm | 2 pm | 3 pm | 4 pm | 5 pm | 6 pm |
| 9.30 | 10.30 | 11.30 | 12.30 | 1.30 | 2.30 | 3.30 | 4.30 | 5.30 | |

Some stores are also open on Saturday mornings 9–1. Museums are open slightly later in high season. Banks are open 9–5 on Fridays. Pharmacies are also open on Saturdays 8–1. Some do open 24hrs but not all. Check first by phoning a division of the tourist office ☎ 427 2623. There is a clinic on 3rd Avenue Bellivill, on the outskirts of Bridgetown, St. Michael which is open until midnight ☎ 228 6120.

DRIVE ON THE
LEFT

TOILETS
FREE

DRIVING

Speed limit on highways: **50mph/80kph**

Speed limit on main roads: **30mph/50kph** (inner city 25mph/40kph)

Speed limit on minor roads: **30mph/50kph**

Must be worn at all times and in rear seats where fitted.

Although there are no specific limits on drinking and driving, you should always drive with due care and attention. You may find that your insurance cover is not valid for accidents due to alcohol.

Fuel is available in leaded, unleaded, premium and diesel. Bridgetown has one 24hr fuel station. Others around the island have varying opening and closing times. Most close on Sundays, so you are advised to fill up before you travel at weekends.

Contact your rental agency and they will either send help or replace the vehicle in the event of a breakdown.

PUBLIC TRANSPORTATION

Internal Flights
There are no internal flights within Barbados. Air LIAT, BWIA, American Eagle, Tropicair, Trans Island Air, Air Martinique and Caribe Express operate flights to neighboring islands in the Caribbean.

Trains
There are no rail services on Barbados.

Buses
Buses are an excellent, inexpensive way of getting around. Frequent services run to most parts of the island. A flat fare of Bds$1.50 takes you anywhere. There are two main types of bus: government-owned (blue with a yellow stripe) for which you must have correct fare, and privately owned mini buses (yellow with a blue stripe) which give change. Destinations are clearly marked on the front or painted on the sides. From Bridgetown, buses run from terminals in Fairchild Street for the south and from Lower Green to the west coast and north. The privately-owned mini buses leave from Probyn Street, River Road and Cheapside terminals. For general enquiries ☎ 436 6820.

Boat Trips
Organized tours of the coastline are available, plus trips to neighboring Caribbean islands (▶ 84–85).

CAR RENTAL

Choose anything from a Mini Moke to an air-conditioned sedan. Rent on arrival at the airport or from your hotel. Vehicles can be hired for an hour, day, week or longer on production of a current driving licence and a major credit card. You must buy a driving permit for Bds$10, issued from the car rental companies or the Ministry of Transport ☎ 427 2623.

CABS

Cabs may be expensive but they can make sense if there are a number of you who want to sightsee or make a journey. Identified by ZR number plates or painted white with a maroon stripe, the cabs are clean, efficient and many have air conditioning. There are no meters, but fares are regulated by the government and published by the tourist office in Bridgetown.

PHOTOGRAPHY

What to photograph: Barbadians dislike having a camera pointed at them. If you must take a photo, ask politely and understand if they refuse. The tourist board has a sightseeing map of the island marked with essential viewpoints.

When to photograph: Early morning, just after sunset and late afternoon are the best times to take pictures as the sunlight is less harsh.

Where to buy film: Although major photography shops in Bridgetown stock many types of film, it is best to bring your own. Remember to pack spare batteries. Take film home to be developed. Pack it in your carry-on bag.

TIPS/GRATUITIES

Yes ✓ No ✗		
Restaurants (10% service included)	✗	
Cafés/bars (10% service included)	✗	
Tour guides	✓	US$10
Hairdressers	✓	US$4
Cabs	✓	US$5
Chambermaids	✓	US$5
Cloakroom attendants	✗	US$4
Toilets	✓	change
Porters	✓	US$4

HEALTH

Doctors
If you fall ill, hotels can arrange a doctor to come and see you. If things get serious, the hospital is never far away on this small island. Full medical insurance is highly recommended and should cover you for medical and hospital costs, transportation to a suitable off-island medical facility if required, repatriation and permanent disability. Note that you will need additional coverage for certain sports such as scuba diving.

Dental Services
Emergency dental treatment can be provided at a cost through a private dentist.

Sun Advice
The Caribbean sun is extremely strong and you must protect your skin. Choose a good-quality, high-factor sunscreen and reapply frequently, especially after swimming and watersports. Avoid the midday sun. Wear good sunglasses and if possible, a wide-brimmed hat. Limit your time in the sun when first going to the beach. If you do suffer sunburn, stay out of the sun until you recover. If symptoms of headache, nausea or dizziness occur, call a doctor.

Drugs
Prescriptions and non-prescription drugs and medicines are available from pharmacies.

Safe Water
Barbados water is very pure, having been filtered by the island's natural coral. It can be enjoyed straight from the tap.

PERSONAL SAFETY

You may be approached and asked to buy marijuana or harder drugs. Politely refuse and walk away. Keep a close eye on belongings and if possible, leave valuables in the hotel safe or room safe. Don't walk the beaches at night and avoid unfamiliar neighborhoods. Don't leave valuables in cars.
Police assistance: ☎ 430 7100 (Emergency ☎ 211 from any call box)

TELEPHONES

Satellite links and direct dialling are available. All local calls are free except from pay-phones where 25 cent coins are needed.

International Dialling Codes
From Barbados to

UK:	0 11 44
Germany:	0 11 49
USA and Canada:	0 11 1
Netherlands:	00 11 31

POST

Postal services are good. The main Post Office is in Cheapside, Bridgetown ☎ 436 4800, open Mon–Fri 7.30–5. Each parish has its own smaller post office and stamps are available from most hotels and book stores.

ELECTRICITY

The power supply in Barbados is 110 volts 50 cycles. Carry an adapter to make sure your appliances fit the two-prong sockets. Alternatively, many hotels can supply adapters.

● A departure tax of Bds$25, or US$12.50, is payable at the check-in counter at the airport when leaving Barbados. If you're on a package holiday, check whether your departure tax has already been paid by the operator.

LANGUAGE

Barbados experienced 300 years of British rule and as a consequence, the official language of the island is English. Everyone speaks and understands English so there is no need to learn the strong and lively West Indian dialect spoken by the local Bajans, and wrongly assumed to be nothing more than broken English. To try to imitate Bajan speak could actually sound false and inappropriate, so it's best to talk normally. Likewise, listening to rapid Bajan speak can be confusing. If you cannot grasp the essence of the conversation, simply ask the speaker to slow down and you'll soon pick-up the essential points. Listening to two Bajans in conversation is fascinating, the sound melodic with a distinct laid-back rhythm.

Visitors who insist on learning a few Bajan words however, can buy Learn to Speak Bajan booklets from some souvenir and bookshops. The dialect is not difficult to learn. Words such as "three" become "tree," the common "the" is shortened to "de," them becomes "dem" and "your" is a spirited "yo" or "yuh." Sometimes the response to a question is a beautifully rich " doan' know child." Whatever language you speak, though, remember always to remain polite. In Barbados, it is common etiquette to say please, thank you and greet people with a cheerful good morning/afternoon/evening.

> **"** Bajan is a dialect which sounds, although it isn't, like broken English. It is a rich, beautiful language all of its own.

Noticeably common is the replacement of "th" with "de," as in:

wid	-	with
den	-	then
dey	-	they
de	-	the
dere	-	there
dese	-	these

Verbs have no participle endings such as -ed, so a Bajan would say 'he fish' instead of "he fished," or "she cook" instead of "she cooked."

Also, the present time is spoken as a real, ongoing thing, for example: "the woman dances to the beat of the steel drum" would be "de woman she dancing to de beat o'de drum." Here are a few wonderful gems to make your ears twitch:

agen	-	again
evaht'ing	-	everything
evaht'ing cook and curry	-	everything's all taken care of
dat ol talk	-	idle gossip
a pot o'Bajan soup	-	a dish of stew
boil up	-	bring to the boil
cook up	-	all ingredients are cooked together
limin	-	hanging around
piece o'pumpkin and piece o'pigtail	-	ingredients for the pot
if greedy wait, hot will cool	-	wait until the dish cools and you can eat
the sea en' got no back door	-	if you get into a mess, you might not get out of it
big bout yah	-	you got fame/money/looks/talent

Acknowledgements

Growing up Stupid Under the Union Jack by Austin Clark. © 1980 by Austin Clarke. Published in Canada by Vintage Canada.

The Automobile Association wishes to thank the following photographers and libraries for their assistance in the preparation of this book.

ANTHONY BLAKE PHOTO LIBRARY (GUY MOBERLY) 52c, (ANTHONY BLAKE) 52b; ELEANOR CHANDLER 9b, 35, 37t, 39b, 51b, 58b, 61b, 66b, 67, 71b, 72; MARY EVANS PICTURE LIBRARY 8b; INTERNATIONAL PHOTOBANK 1, 10b, 15b, 37b, 69b, 73b; MOUNT GAY DISTILLERY 50b, 50/51; PICTURES COLOUR LIBRARY 70; POWERSTOCK/ZEFA 59b; REX FEATURES 8b, 10b; WORLD PICTURES 16b, 19b

The remaining photographs are held in the Association's own library (AA PHOTO LIBRARY) and were taken by Lee Karen Stow with the exception of the following: Peter Baker 5t, 6t, 7t, 8t, 9t, 10t, 11b, 24b, 27, 41, 45b, 53b, 87b

Copy editor: Rebecca Snelling Verifier: Simon Martin
Editorial management: Apostrophe S Limited

Dear Essential Traveller

**Your comments, opinions and recommendations are very
important to us. So please help us to improve our travel
guides by taking a few minutes to complete this simple
questionnaire.**

*You do not need a stamp (unless posted outside the UK). If you do not want to cut this page
from your guide, then photocopy it or write your answers on a plain sheet of paper.*

Send to: **The Editor, AA World Travel Guides,
FREEPOST SCE 4598, Basingstoke RG21 4GY.**

Your recommendations...

We always encourage readers' recommendations for restaurants, nightlife
or shopping – if your recommendation is used in the next edition of the
guide, we will send you a *FREE* AA *Essential* **Guide** of your choice.
Please state below the establishment name, location and your reasons
for recommending it.

_____

_____

_____

_____

Please send me **AA *Essential*** _____

About this guide...

Which title did you buy?
    AA *Essential* _____

Where did you buy it? _____

When? m m / y y

Why did you choose an AA *Essential* Guide? _____

_____

_____

_____

_____

Did this guide meet your expectations?
    Exceeded ☐   Met all ☐   Met most ☐   Fell below ☐

    Please give your reasons _____

_____

_____

_____

continued on next page...

Were there any aspects of this guide that you particularly liked? _____

_____

_____

Is there anything we could have done better? _____

_____

_____

About you...

Name (*Mr/Mrs/Ms*) _____

    Address _____

_____

    _____ Postcode _____

    Daytime tel nos _____

Please only give us your mobile phone number if you wish to hear from us about other products and services from the AA and partners by text or mms.

Which age group are you in?
    Under 25 ☐ 25–34 ☐ 35–44 ☐ 45–54 ☐ 55–64 ☐ 65+ ☐

How many trips do you make a year?
    Less than one ☐ One ☐ Two ☐ Three or more ☐

Are you an AA member? Yes ☐ No ☐

About your trip...

When did you book? m m / y y   When did you travel? m m / y y
How long did you stay? _____
Was it for business or leisure? _____
Did you buy any other travel guides for your trip?
    If yes, which ones? _____

Thank you for taking the time to complete this questionnaire. Please send it to us as soon as possible, and remember, you do not need a stamp (*unless posted outside the UK*).

Happy Holidays!

The Atlas

Acknowledgements
All pictures are from AA World Travel Library with contributions from the following photographers:
Peter Baker: boat on beach, dancing girl, market produce, roadside dominoes
Lee Karen Stow: stilt walker, children on a beach

www.theAA.com
The Automobile Association's website offers comprehensive and up-to-the-minute information covering AA-approved hotels, guest houses and B&Bs, restaurants and pubs in the UK; airport parking, insurance, breakdown cover, European motoring advice, a ferry planner, European route planner, overseas fuel prices, a bookshop and much more.

www.aaa.com
AAA's website offers comprehensive information covering AAA-approved hotels and restaurants in the US. In addition, AAA can assist US citizens with obtaining a passport, reservations and tickets for cruise, tour, motorcoach, rail and air travel. AAA provides information on independent or escorted tours for individuals or groups and offers benefits on cruises, tours and travel packages.

The Foreign and Commonwealth Office
Country advice, traveller's tips, before you
go information, checklists and more.
www.fco.gov.uk

Barbados Tourism Authority
www.barbados.org

GENERAL
UK Passport Service
www.ukpa.gov.uk

US passport information
www.travel.state.gov

Health Advice for Travellers
www.doh.gov.uk/traveladvice

BBC—Holiday
www.bbc.co.uk/holiday

The Full Universal Currency Converter
www.xe.com/ucc/full.shtml

Flying with Kids
www.flyingwithkids.com

www.caribbean-on-line.com
www.funbarbados.com
www.netcarib.com/barbados

TRAVEL
Flights and Information
www.cheapflights.co.uk
www.thisistravel.co.uk
www.ba.com
www.worldairportguide.com

Dual carriageway with motorway characteristics Autobahnähnliche Schnellstraße	Church • Chapel Kirche • Kapelle
Highway Fernverkehrsstraße	Castle • Ruin Burg • Ruine
Important main road Wichtige Hauptstraße	Point of interest • Nature sight Sehenswürdigkeit • Naturattraktio
Main road Hauptstraße	Windmill • Cave Windmühle • Höhle
Secondary road Nebenstraße	Hotel • Plantation house Hotel • Plantagenhaus
Carriageway • Path Fahrweg • Pfad	Wildlife reserve • Riding Wildgehege • Reiten
1,4/2,3 Distance in miles/km Entfernung in miles/km	Lighthouse • Radio Tower Leuchtturm • Funkturm
Parish boundary Kirchengemeindegrenzen	Picnic area • Shipwreck Picknick • Schiffswrack
Int. Airport • Harbour Int. Flughafen • Hafen	Beach • Yachting Strand • Segelsport
Museum • Monument Museum • Denkmal	Deap sea fishing • Scuba diving Hochseefischen • Sporttauchen
Synagogue • Market Synagoge • Markt	Parasailing • Windsurfing Paragleiten • Windsurfen
Information • Police Information • Polizei	Golf • National park Golf • Nationalpark
Post office • Hospital Postamt • Krankenhaus	Petrol station Tankstelle

```
0        1        2       3 km
0            1           2 miles
```

Maps © MAIRDUMONT / Falk Verlag 2005

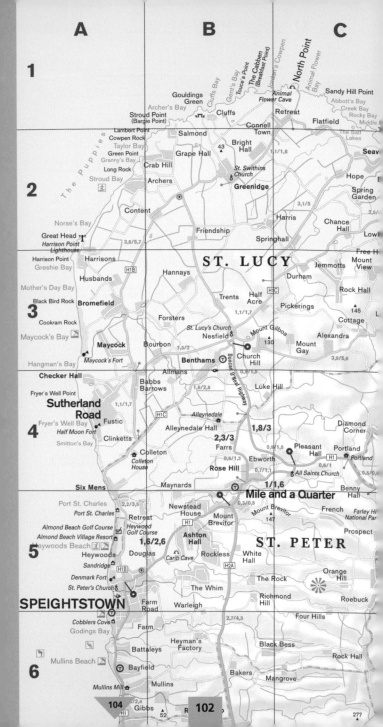

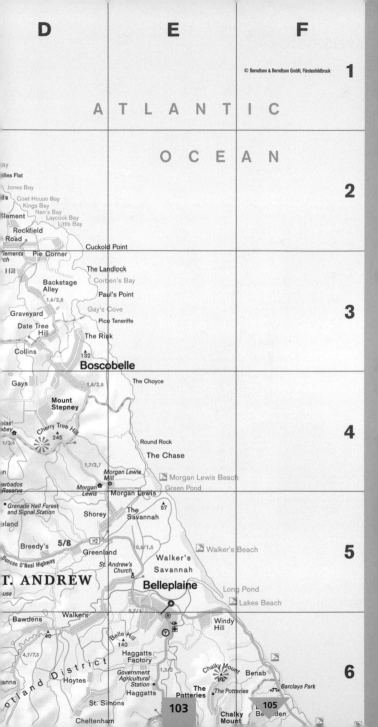

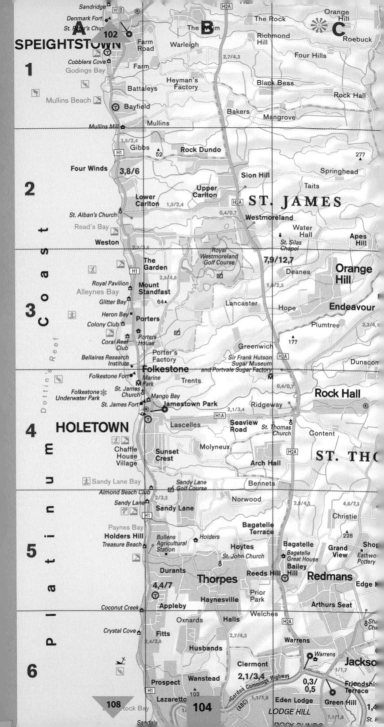

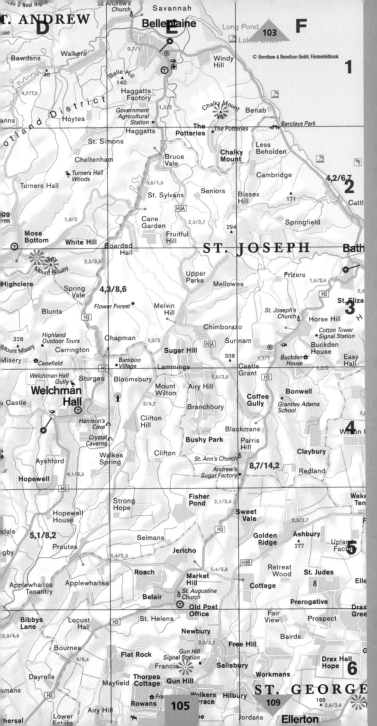

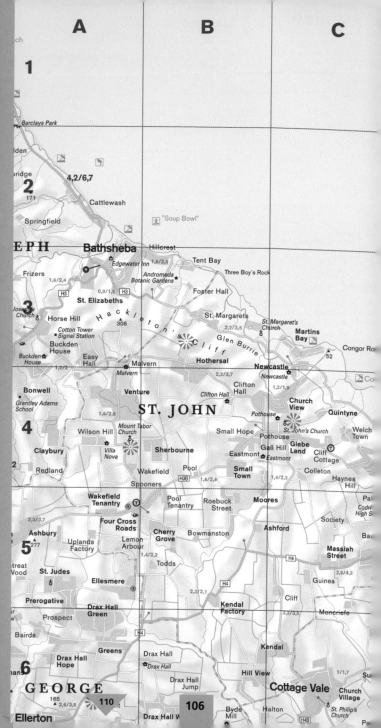

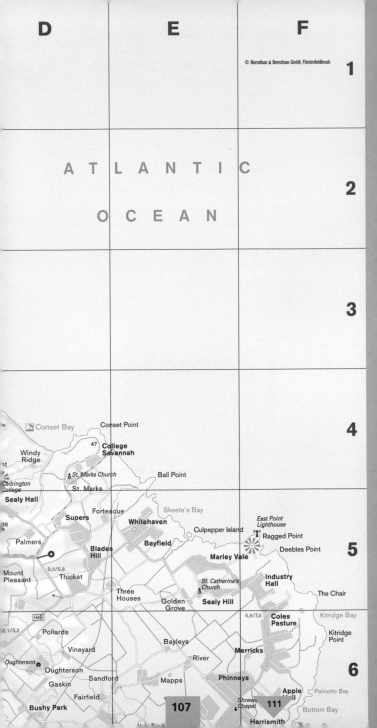

D   **E**   **F**

1

A T L A N T I C

O C E A N

2

3

4

🖼 Conset Bay

Conset Point

Windy
Ridge

47 **College
Savannah**

Ball Point

⚓St. Marks Church

Codrington
College

St. Marks

Sealy Hall

Fortescue

Skeete's Bay

Supers

Whitehaven

Culpepper Island

East Point
Lighthouse

🚨 Ragged Point

Palmers

Bayfield

**Blades
Hill**

Marley Vale

Deebles Point

0,5/0,8

5

Mount
Pleasant

Thicket

St. Catherine's
⚓Church

**Industry
Hall**

The Chair

Three
Houses

Golden
Grove

Sealy Hill

4,9/7,8

Kitridge Bay

H48

**Coles
Pasture**

2,1/3,2

Pollards

Bayleys

Kitridge
Point

Vineyard

Merricks

Oughterson 🏠

Oughterson

River

Gaskin

Sandford

Mapps

Phinneys

Apple

Palmetto Bay

Fairfield

Bushy Park

Shrews
⚓Chapel

111

Bottom Bay

Harrismith

6

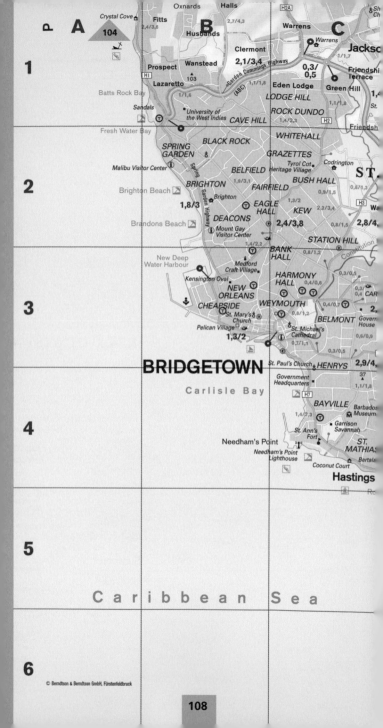

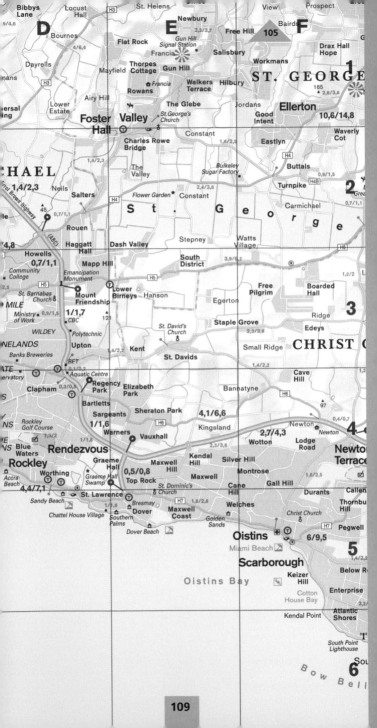

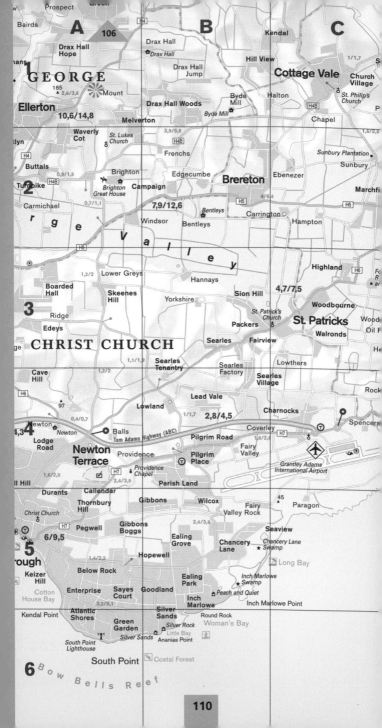

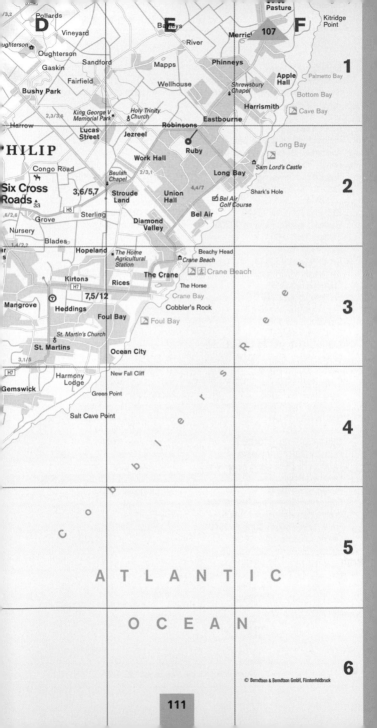

Sight Locator Index

This index relates to the atlas section on pages 102–111 and the inside front and back covers. We have given map references to the main sights of interest in the book. Some sights in the index may not be plotted on the atlas.

For the main index see pages 125–126